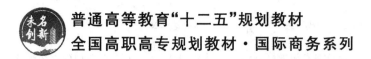

普通高等教育"十二五"规划教材
全国高职高专规划教材·国际商务系列

国际商务英语

International Business English

周欣奕 主编

内 容 简 介

本书是一本以工作任务为导向的国际商务英语教材,全书以一家跨国公司的国际销售部门的一名新员工在国际商务岗位的工作过程为线索来设置工作任务,包括岗位申请、岗位面试、新员工入职、公司和产品、部门例会、客户接待、商务谈判和商务函件 8 个工作模块。通过测试案例导入工作模块,布置工作任务并提出任务要求,指导学生按照任务要求分步骤通过模拟演练完成工作流程,然后辅以国际商务的相关知识要点,最后通过听、说、读、写等各方面的技能训练,达到技能要求。本书难易适中,语言素材规范,符合实际工作任务。

本书适用于高职层次的国际商务专业、商务英语专业、国际贸易专业,也可用于其他商贸类专业人员的自学用书。

图书在版编目(CIP)数据

国际商务英语/周欣奕主编. —北京:北京大学出版社,2013.7
(全国高职高专规划教材·国际商务系列)
ISBN 978-7-301-21931-7

Ⅰ. ①国… Ⅱ. ①周… Ⅲ. ①国际商务－英语－高等职业教育－教材 Ⅳ. ①H31

中国版本图书馆 CIP 数据核字(2013)第 004692 号

书　　　　名:国际商务英语
著作责任者:周欣奕　主编
策 划 编 辑:温丹丹
责 任 编 辑:温丹丹
标 准 书 号:ISBN 978-7-301-21931-7/F·3476
出 版 发 行:北京大学出版社
地　　　　址:北京市海淀区成府路 205 号　100871
网　　　　址:http://www.pup.cn　新浪官方微博:@北京大学出版社
电 子 信 箱:zyjy@pup.cn
电　　　　话:邮购部 62752015　发行部 62750672　编辑部 62765126　出版部 62754962
印 刷 者:北京富生印刷厂
经 销 者:新华书店
　　　　　787 毫米×1092 毫米　16 开本　12.75 印张　304 千字
　　　　　2013 年 7 月第 1 版　2013 年 7 月第 1 次印刷
定　　　　价:30.00 元(含光盘)

未经许可,不得以任何方式复制或抄袭本书之部分或全部内容。
版权所有,侵权必究
举报电话:010-62752024　电子信箱:fd@pup.pku.edu.cn

前言
Preface

本书是一本以工作任务为导向的国际商务英语教材。

在经济全球化的进程中,各类企业需要越来越多具有国际思维习惯和跨文化交际能力的国际商务人才。这就对高职国际商务英语课程的教学设计和教学内容提出了更高的要求。本书是在课程改革的基础上,以实践为核心、以岗位需求为依据、以提高高职国际商务英语能力为目标、以工作过程为导向、以企业真实任务为载体开发出来的。

本书以一家跨国公司的国际销售部门的一名新员工在国际商务岗位的工作过程为线索来设置工作任务。通过模拟跨国企业真实场景,营造国际语言环境,使学生亲自经历结构完整的国际商务工作过程,并培养学生诚实、守信、善于沟通和合作的品质。

本书包括岗位申请、岗位面试、新员工入职、公司和产品、部门例会、客户接待、商务谈判和商务函件8个工作模块。每个模块由导入案例、任务要求、任务流程、知识要点、技能要求5个部分组成。

其中,导入案例通过自我测试引导学生进入模块主题,使学生在了解自己的基础上,更好地完成工作任务。任务要求是对任务进行详细描述,提供相关任务背景,并指导学生分配角色。学生可以根据任务要求进行模拟演练,完成工作任务。任务流程则提供了参考模板,学生完成任务后可以对照任务流程,在老师的指导下分析得失。知识要点是在学生完成任务的过程中进行的国际商务专业知识指导,并配有相应的练习。技能要求则通过词汇强化以及听、说、读、写等多方面的技能训练,来加强学生的英语语言沟通能力。

在本书编写过程中得到北京财贸职业学院国际教育学院潘勇院长、财贸素养部王莉莉副教授、科研处田志英副教授、工商系诸位老师以及出版社同仁的大力支持和帮助,在此由衷表示感谢。

由于编者水平所限,书中难免有不妥之处,敬请指正。

周欣奕
2013年4月

本教材配有教学课件,如有老师需要,请加QQ群(279806670)或发电子邮件至zyjy@pup.cn索取,也可致电北京大学出版社:010-62765126。

目 录
Contents

Module One	Application for an International Business Job	1
Module Two	Interviewing for an International Business Job	22
Module Three	Working Environment	44
Module Four	Company and Product	61
Module Five	Regular Meeting	83
Module Six	Customer Reception	106
Module Seven	Business Negotiation	123
Module Eight	Business Correspondence	140
Appendix		168
References		196

Module One

Application for an International Business Job

导入案例

职业性格测试。

任务要求

学生分成三人一组，分别扮演应聘者、招聘公司人力资源部经理，招聘岗位所在部门经理，用英文完成招聘广告、应聘信和简历、公司内部讨论候选人名单等任务。

任务流程

1. 人力资源部经理在网络上发布招聘广告。
2. 应聘者根据招聘广告写一封附有简历的求职信。
3. 人力资源部经理收到求职信和简历后，发备忘录给岗位所在部门经理征询意见。部门经理回复备忘录给人力资源部经理，同意对应聘者进行面试。

知识要点

1. 国际商务。
2. 国际销售代表。

技能要求

1. 词汇：缩略词。
2. 听：招聘广告。
3. 说：写申请信的注意事项。
4. 读：销售部经理岗位介绍。
5. 写：申请信。

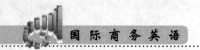

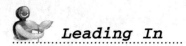

Leading In

Personality Test [1]

Answer honestly, and for who you are NOW... not who you may have been in the past. Have pen or pencil and paper ready. This is a real test given by the Human Relations Dept. at many major corporations today. It helps them get better insight concerning their employees and prospective employees.

It's only 10 simple questions, so... grab a pencil and paper and keep track of your letter answers.

1. When do you feel your best?

A. In the morning.

B. During the afternoon and early evening.

C. Late at night.

2. You usually walk...

A. Fairly fast, with long steps

B. Fairly fast, with little steps

C. Less fast, head up, looking the world in the face

D. Less fast, head down

E. Very slowly

3. When talking to people you...

A. Stand with your arms folded

B. Have your hands clasped

C. Have one or both your hands on your hips

D. Touch or push the person to whom you are talking

E. Play with your ear, touch your chin, or smooth your hair

4. When relaxing, you sit with...

A. Your knees bent with your legs neatly side by side

B. Your legs crossed

C. Your legs stretched out or straight

D. One leg curled under you

5. When something really amuses you, you react with...

A. Big appreciated laugh

B. A laugh, but not a loud one

C. A quiet chuckle

---

1. Based on hsnfsteven.wikispaces.com/file/view/E)+personality+test.doc.

Module One Application for an International Business Job

D. A sheepish smile

6. When you go to a party or social gathering you...

A. Make a loud entrance so everyone notices you

B. Make a quiet entrance, looking around for someone you know

C. Make the quietest entrance, trying to stay unnoticed

7. You're working very hard, concentrating hard, and you're interrupted...

A. Welcome the break

B. Feel extremely irritated

C. Vary between these two extremes

8. Which of the following colors do you like most?

A. Red or orange

B. Black

C. Yellow or light blue

D. Green

E. Dark blue or purple

F. White

G. Brown or gray

9. When you are in bed at night, in those last few moments before going to sleep....

A. Stretched out on your back

B. Stretched out face down on your stomach

C. On your side, slightly curled

D. With your head on one arm

E. With your head under the covers

10. You often dream that you are...

A. Falling

B. Fighting or struggling

C. Searching for something or somebody

D. Flying or floating

E. You usually have dreamless sleep

F. Your dreams are always pleasant

POINTS:

1. A. 2 B. 4 C. 6

2. A. 6 B. 4 C. 7 D. 2 E. 1

3. A. 4 B. 2 C. 5 D. 7 E. 6

4. A. 4 B. 6 C. 2 D. 1

5. A. 6 B. 4 C. 3 D. 5 E. 1

6. A. 6 B. 4 C. 2

7. A. 6 B. 2 C. 1

8. A. 6 B. 7 C. 5 D. 4 E. 3 F. 2 G. 1

9. A. 7 B. 6 C. 4 D. 2 E. 1
10. A. 4 B. 2 C. 3 D. 5 E. 6 F. 1

Now add up the total number of points.

The students are divided into groups with 3 members each. Student A plays a role as an applicant. Student B plays a role as the HR manager. And student C plays a role as the manager of the department for which the applicant is applying. They will finish the tasks together as follows.

Task 1 Writing a Job Advertisement

A job description is a document primarily used by employers as an advertisement for prospective employees which provide applicants with a comprehensive summary of the necessary skills, abilities, experience and qualifications that are required to perform the duties of the position. It also can be used for determining compensation and performance reviews. It includes job title, job objectives, main job tasks and responsibilities, education and experience, and key competencies.

A job advertisement is placed when a vacancy arises within a company or organization. Job advertisements can be found in newspapers, online and on notice boards at companies. A job advertisement should focus on the person a company is trying to attract and the details of the job vacancy. A Job Advertisement will provide the name of the company, the basic details of the company, the position provided, the brief qualification that are required, the compensation, the nominated contact person and contact method.

Student B plays a role as Bridges Thompson, the HR manager of Rainbow Pet Products Co., Ltd., Los Angeles, California, which is specialized in Pet Products.

The Rainbow Pet Products Co., Ltd., Los Angeles, California is going to explore Asian Market especially in China. They are in urgent need of international salespersons who are familiar with Asian Culture. Bridges Thompson writes a job advertisement according to the job description (Table 1-1) in order to find an international salesperson who can obtain USD 1.5k each month plus commission with 2-weeks vacation, 10 paid holidays for the International Sales Department.

The company's address: 1358 Westwood Blvd, Los Angeles, CA90024-4911. Telephone number: 213-345-9109.

Fax number: 213-345-9108.

E-mail address: bridgesthompson@yahoo.com.

Module One *Application for an International Business Job*

Table 1-1 Job Description

Job Description
Job Title: International Salesperson
General Purpose: To plan and carry out international sales activities on assigned areas. Responsible for ensuring customer satisfaction and managing quality of product and service delivery.
Main Job Tasks and Responsibilities: To make international market research and surveys To develop and maintain a customer database and promotional materials To schedule and conduct international sales and marketing activity To make international sales calls to new or existing clients To develop and make presentations of company products and services to current and potential clients To respond to international sales inquiries and concerns by phone, electronically or in person To negotiate with international clients To fulfill international sales contracts To ensure customer service satisfaction and good client relationships To follow up on international sales activity and service delivery To perform quality checks on product To maintain international sales activity records and prepare sales reports
Education and Experience: College degree Majored in international business or marketing 2 years experience in sales
Key Competencies: Persuasiveness, adaptability, stress tolerance Verbal and written communication skills Negotiation skills

 Write a job advertisement with the following information.

- Company Name
- Job title
- Draw Attention sentence and company introduction
- Necessary Requirements
- Compensation
- Contact Method

(150-200 words)

```
                        _____

                                Requires
                            _____

        _____
        _____
        _____
        _____
        _____

        For consideration submit cover letter and resume to: _____
        _____
        Address: _____
        Tel: _____
        Fax: _____
        E-mail: _____
        Contact: _____
```

Task 2 Writing an Application Letter with a CV/Résumé

When you apply for a job, you'll generally be asked to send in your CV/résumé together with a letter or an email of application.

A CV or résumé is a brief account of your previous employment, education, and qualifications. It includes personal information, objective, work experience, education, achievements & awards, computer and language skills, and personal qualities. Name, sex, age, and contact method should be introduced in the personal information. Objective tells what kind of position you are looking for. Work experience contains previous working experience and previous positions and the level of responsibility required by those positions. Education contains the name and location of the universities that you have graduated, the graduation year, and what degrees you have obtained, if necessary, the relevant courses you have attended for this specific position. Achievements & awards involve what you have been awarded or what you have achieved on campus or in previous work. You should mention your ability to operate a computer, especially the computer languages and programs you are familiar with. You should also mention the languages you know, specify the level of knowledge involved: satisfactory, good, or excellent. And then the personalities should be told at last.

Module One Application for an International Business Job

Write your application in a letter format with letter head, inside address, salutation, body of the letter, complimentary close and signature. Clearly identify the position you are applying for in your application. And address how your skills, abilities, experience and qualifications meet the requirements. Pay attention to each selection criterion which is derived from the requirements and duties specified in the job description. Employers often receive hundreds of applications for a job, so it's very important to make sure that your CV/resumé and job application letter create the right impression and present your personal information in a focused, well-structured, and attractive way.

Student A plays a role as Daniel Zheng, who was born in May 15th, 2008. He comes from China. He is an international student majored in international business in American Commercial College, Shreveport. He has been worked as a salesperson for Cool Ice-cream House for two years.

Daniel Zheng reads the job advertisement of Rainbow Pet Products Co., Ltd., Los Angeles, California online. He is going to apply for the job as an international salesperson. He writes a CV/resumé together with an application letter on Sept. 12th, 2012 with envelope according to the above Job Description (Table 1-1) and the Job advertisement written by Bridges Thompson.

Daniel Zheng's address: 3014 Knight St. Shreveport, LA 71105.
Mobile phone number: 866-8736-5632.
Fax number: 318-861-2119.
The E-mail address: danielzheng@yahoo.com.

 Fill in the CV/resumé with the above information.

CURRICULUM VITAE
Personal Information:
Name:
Date of Birth:
Sex:
Martial Status:
Nationality:
Address:
Telephone:
E-mail:
Fax:
Job objectives:

Work Experience:
Aug., 2010—present:

Education:
Aug., 2007—Aug., 2010:

Achievements & Awards:
Achieved and carried out several promotion activities last summer.
Awarded as the Employee of the 2011 Award of the Cool Ice-cream House
Abilities and Skills:
Skilled in use of MS, Win 95/NT
Personal Qualities:

Write an application letter containing the following information with the help of the above CV/résumé.

- The objectives of the letter and the information channel
- Education and Experience
- Skills and qualification to meet the requirements
- Enclosing the CV/résumé and expressing thanks

(150-200 words)

Daniel Zheng
3014 Knight St. Shreveport, LA 71105, USA
Tel: 866-8736-5632
Fax: 318-861-2119
E-mail: danielzheng@yahoo.com

Sept. 12, 2012

Bridges Thompson
Manager of HR Department
Rainbow Pet Products Co., Ltd., Los Angeles, California.
1358 Westwood Blvd
Los Angeles, CA90024-4911
USA

Gentlemen:

Sincerely yours,
Daniel Zheng
Daniel Zheng

Enc.: CV

Module One   Application for an International Business Job

 Finish the envelope of the application letter with the following information.
- Name and address of the sender
- Name and address of the receiver

```
┌─────────────────────────────────────────────────┐
│                                    ┌─────────┐  │
│                                    │ Stamps  │  │
│                                    │         │  │
│                                    └─────────┘  │
│                                                 │
│                                                 │
│                                                 │
│                                                 │
│                                                 │
│                                                 │
│                                                 │
│                                                 │
│                                                 │
└─────────────────────────────────────────────────┘
```

Task 3   Writing a Memo

A memorandum (Memo) is a document typically used for communication within a company. Memos can be as formal as a business letter and used to present a report. However, the heading and overall tone make a memo different from a business letter. Because you generally send memos to co-workers and colleagues, you do not have to include a formal salutation or closing remark.

Student B plays a role as Bridges Thompson, the HR manager of Rainbow Pet Products Co., Ltd., Los Angeles, California.

Student C plays a role as Christine Winters, the manager of International Sales Department of Rainbow Pet Products Co., Ltd., Los Angeles, California.

After receiving four application letters including Daniel Zheng's, Bridges Thompson writes a memo attached the application letters and CVs/résumés to Christine Winters on Sept. 20th, 2012 and asks her opinion on the interview candidates in order to make arrangements for the interview.

Christine Winters has received the memo from Bridges Thompson. After evaluating the application letters and CVs/résumés, she recommends Daniel Zheng as the interview candidate and tells the reasons by writing a memo to Bridges Thompson on Sept. 22nd, 2012. The decision of whether to interview an applicant is based on how well the applicant has met the requirements.

Write a memo with the following information.
- Attached information
- Ask for recommendation
- Future Arrangement
- Express thanks

(50-100 words)

MEMO
To
From
Date
Subject

 Write a memo with the following information.
- Requirements for the position
- Recommendation
- Reasons
- Ask the date and time of the interview
- Express thanks

(50-100 words)

MEMO
To
From
Date
Subject

Module One   *Application for an International Business Job*

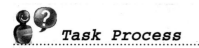

Task 1   Writing a Job Advertisement

<u>   Rainbow Pet Products Co., Ltd., Los Angeles, California   </u>
Requires
<u>   International Salespersons   </u>

    <u>If you love to search for new business opportunities, why not join the international sales team at the Rainbow Pet Products Co., Ltd., Los Angeles, California? We are specialized in Pet Products in USA. We are going to explore Asian market. We are a stable company, with excellent benefits, outstanding co-workers, and a fun work environment. Are you a persuasive, goal driven person who is familiar with Asian culture and has experience in sales? We want you! You can earn USD 1.5k each month plus commission with 2-week vacation, 10 days paid holidays. Apply now. Your office is waiting.</u>

    For consideration submit cover letter and resume to: <u>HR department, Rainbow Pet Products Co., Ltd., Los Angeles, California.</u>
    Address: <u>1358 Westwood Blvd, Los Angeles, CA90024-4911</u>
    Tel: <u>213-345-9109</u>
    Fax: <u>213-345-9108</u>
    E-mail: <u>bridgesthompson@yahoo.com</u>
    Contact: <u>Bridges Thompson</u>

Task 2   Writing an Application Letter with a CV/Résumé

CURRICULUM VITAE
Personal Information:
Name: Daniel Zheng
Date of Birth: May 15, 1988
Sex: Male
Martial Status: Single
Nationality: Chinese
Address: 3014 Knight St. Shreveport, LA 71105
Telephone: 866-8736-5632
Fax: 318-861-2119
E-mail: danielzheng@yahoo.com.
Job objectives:
International Salesperson

11

Work Experience:
Aug., 2010-present: a salesperson for Cool Ice-cream House
Education:
Aug., 2007-Aug., 2010: international student in American Commercial College, majored in International Business
Achievements & Awards:
Achieved and carried out several promotion activities last summer.
Awarded as the Employee of the 2011 Award
Abilities and Skills:
I'm skilled in use of MS, Win 95/NT
My native language is Chinese.
I am familiar with Chinese culture.
Personal Qualities:
Persuasive, outgoing with coordination skills, teamwork spirit, Hard-working

Daniel Zheng
3014 Knight St. Shreveport, LA 71105, USA
Tel: 866-8736-5632
Fax: 318-861-2119
E-mail: danielzheng@yahoo.com.

Sept. 12th, 2012

Bridges Thompson
Manager of HR Department
Rainbow Pet Products Co., Ltd., Los Angeles, California.
1358 Westwood Blvd
Los Angeles, CA90024-4911
USA

Gentlemen:

I am writing to apply for the position of international salesperson which was advertised on the internet.

I come from China. I have a college diploma from the American Commercial College. My major is International Business. For the past two years, I have worked as a salesperson for Cool Ice-cream House.

I have the knowledge of sales, and customer service, and I am skilled in organizing meetings, making presentations, writing reports and dealing with customers. I am skilled in use of MS, Win 95/NT. My native language is Chinese and I'm familiar with Chinese culture. I have two years of sales experience and I achieved and carried out several promotion activities last summer and I was awarded as the Employee of the 2011 Award. I feel I would be especially qualified to work in this position because of my interest and experience in sales and marketing. My excellent communication skills would be a definite asset for your company.

Module One Application for an International Business Job

I am enclosing a copy of my CV and will gladly provide any further information you may require. I would welcome the opportunity of discussing your needs and my experience and abilities.

Sincerely yours,
Daniel Zheng
Daniel Zheng

Enc.: CV

Danial Zheng
3014 Knight St. Shreveport
LA 71105
USA

Stamps

Bridges Thompson
Manager of HR Department
Rainbow Pet Products Co., Ltd., Los Angeles, California.
1358 Westwood Blvd
Los Angeles, CA90024-4911
USA

Task 3 Writing a Memo

MEMO
To Christine Winters, International Sales Manager
From Bridges Thompson, HR Manager
Date Sept. 20th, 2012
Subject Applicants for International Salesperson

Attached are the application letters and CVs/résumés of four applicants who have applied for your department position.

Please evaluate these applicants and then recommend a person you want to interview to me as soon as possible.

When I have the names, I will make arrangements for the interviews.

Thanks a lot.

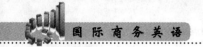

MEMO
To Bridges Thompson, HR Manager
From Christine Winters, International Sales Manager
Date Sept. 22nd, 2012
Subject Recommendation

As this position requires excellent communication skills, it is important to have the sales experience.

After evaluating these applicants, I'd like to recommend Daniel Zheng. His excellent achievement and awards in the sales experience is impressing. And his Chinese background is absolutely an advantage for the position. He would be a definite asset for our company.

If he is available, please let me have the date and time of interview.

Thank you for your help.

International Business

International business consists of transactions that are carried out across national borders to satisfy the objectives of individuals, companies, and organizations. Primary types of international business are international trade and foreign direct investment. The latter is carried out in varied forms, including wholly owned subsidiaries and joint ventures. Additional types of international business are licensing, franchising and management contracts.

International trade is the exchange of goods or services along international borders. This type of trade allows for a greater competition and more competitive pricing in the market. The competition results in more affordable products for the consumer. The exchange of goods also affects the economy of the world as dictated by supply and demand, making goods and services obtainable which may not otherwise be available to consumers globally.

Foreign direct investment (FDI) is a kind of investment directly into production in a country by a company located in another country, either by buying a company in the target country or by expanding operations of an existing business in that country. Foreign direct investment is done for many reasons including to take advantage of cheaper wages in the country, special investment privileges such as tax exemptions offered by the country as an incentive to gain tariff-free access to the markets of the country or the region.

A license is an authorization (by the licensor) to use the licensed material (by the licensee). In particular a license may be issued by authorities, to allow an activity that would otherwise be forbidden. It may require paying a fee and/or proving a capability. The requirement may also serve to keep the authorities informed on a type of activity, and to give them the opportunity to set conditions and limitations.

Franchise is the practice of using another firm's successful business model. For the franchisor, the franchise is an alternative to building "chain stores" to distribute goods that avoids the investments and liability of a chain.

Contract management is the process of systematically and efficiently managing contract creation, execution, and analysis for the purpose of maximizing financial and operational performance and minimizing risk.

International Business causes the flow of ideas, services, and capital across the world. International business provides challenging employment opportunities, reallocates resources, makes preferential choices, and shifts activities to a global level. It can offer consumers new choices. It can also permit the acquisition of a wider variety of products, and facilitate the mobility of labor, capital, and technology.

Practice: Fill A-L into Column II.

I Types of international Business	II Activities
International Trade	
FDI	
License	
Franchise	
Contract management	

A. To acquire shares in a foreign enterprise
B. To buy an intellectual property
C. To merge an unrelated enterprise
D. To open a Subway Restaurant
E. To distribute products under a trademark in a foreign country in a period time
F. To amend the implementation or execution of foreign employee contract.
G. To import textiles
H. To open a 7-Eleven in China
I. To install a software on a computer with a unique code in other country
J. To own a wholly-owned subsidiaries in a foreign country
K. To export cars
L. To participate in the activities of a Joint Venture

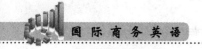

International Salesperson

International Salesperson deals with discovering customer needs, and determining product solutions. This is the person who calls on clients, makes offers and concludes individual deals for sales of the company's products. This often involves writing proposals or coordinating bids for competitive tenders. Alternatively an international salesperson may coordinate the operations of local distributors.

International Salesperson requires excellent interpersonal skills, backed up by a good understanding of the business culture in the target market. But the ability to make a good impression is only the first part of the sales job. Negotiating and sales skills are ultimately directed towards the need to close the deal. This requires practical business sense. International Salesperson also requires good written and oral communications skills and must be computer literate. Fluency in the languages of target markets may be required.

International salesperson should enjoy working with people, especially people from different cultures and should have outgoing personalities. They often work alone, but must also possess team skills. Since they must meet sales targets, and are often paid commissions, they need to be self-starters.

Practice: Match column I with column II.

I Position	II Responsibilities
1. Sales Persons	A. To attend to visitors and deal with inquiries on the phone and face to face. Supply information regarding the organization to the general public, clients and customers.
2. Receptionist	B. To involve both the export and import of goods and services.
3. Secretary	C. To be responsible for maintaining document design consistency for all documents related to the international business.
4. International Salesperson	D. To plan and carry out all sales activities on assigned accounts or areas. Responsible for ensuring customer satisfaction and managing quality of product and service delivery.
5. Documentation Specialist	E. To provide personal administrative support to management and the company through conducting and organizing administrative duties and activities including receiving and handling information.

Module One Application for an International Business Job

Skills Requirements

Vocabulary: Abbrieviation

 Guess the meanings of the following abbreviation and finish the sentences.

abbr.	English	Chinese	Abbr.	English	Chinese
1. ad.			11. Co.		
2. m-f			12. corp		
3. dept.			13. P/T		
4. Jr.			14. F/T		
5. Sr.			15. temp.		
6. Wpm			16. perm.		
7. ref			17. k		
8. blvd			18. Ave.		
9. O/T			19. Fr. Ben.		
10. CV			20. etc.		

1. He is responsible for checking and calculating staff for their _____.
2. He opened a fashion house in the Fifth _____.
3. Virtually all of the _____ managers at our company were promoted from _____ managers within.
4. His future is closely bound up with that of the _____.
5. I learned about it from your _____ in the newspaper.
6. In only a few weeks, my average reading speed went from roughly 300 _____, to over 800.
7. EDC _____ and DHF _____, were amalgamated into a _____.
8. Candidate shall send a letter of application with a _____ to the HR manager.
9. You can work anytime for 1-3 hours a day, _____. Or You can get 3 working days a week as long as you can do equivalent task.
10. Do you have skills (musician, carpenter, writer, _____) that you can use to get some part time jobs?
11. The applicant provides a portfolio of work, _____, and arranges for a preliminary screening (probably a phone interview).

12. Whether it's a _____ or _____ job, embrace it.
13. Next to each _____ is its location and the name of the manager.
14. Most of the workers who work _____ came from all over the country.
15. I have a _____ and stable job here.
16. The store is located on Sunset _____ in West Hollywood.

Listening: Job Advertisement

Listen to the Job Advertisement twice, and complete the following notes with no more than 10 words for each blank according to what you have listened.

Company Name	
Job Title	
Products	
Education required	
Experience required	
The Salary	
Contact person	

Speaking: Tips for Writing an Application Letter

Work in pairs with a partner. Look at the question. Take one minute to prepare your answer. Think of reasons to explain your choice. Then tell your partner your answer and reasons.

WHAT IS IMPORTANT WHEN ...?
Writing an application letter
- Find out as much as you can about the job before writing
- Check spelling and watch your grammar
- Write neatly

Module One — Application for an International Business Job

Reading: Job Description

Read the Job Description below about a Sales Manager. Choose the correct word (A, B or C) to fill each gap.

JOB DESCRIPTION FOR A SALES MANAGER [1]

General Purpose:
Responsible for planning, implementing and directing the sales <u>1._____</u> of the company in a designated area to achieve sales <u>2._____</u>

Main Job Tasks and Responsibilities:
To develop a sales strategy to achieve organizational sales goals and revenues
To set individual sales targets with sales team
To delegate responsibility for customer accounts to sales personnel
To co-ordinate sales action plans for individual salespeople
To oversee the activities and performance of the sales team
To ensure sales team have the necessary resources to perform properly
To monitor the <u>3._____</u> of sales objectives by the sales team
To liaise with other company functions to ensure achievement of sales objectives
To evaluate <u>4._____</u> of sales staff
To provide feedback, support and coaching to the sales team
To plan and direct sales team training
To assist with the development of sales presentations and proposals
To investigate lost sales and customer accounts
To track, collate and interpret sales figures
To forecast annual, <u>5._____</u> and monthly sales revenue
To generate timely sales reports
To develop pricing schedules and rates
To formulate sales policies and procedures
To help prepare budgets
To control <u>6._____</u> and monitor budgets
To maintain inventory control
To conduct market research and competitor and customer analysis
To analyse data to identify sales opportunities
To develop promotional ideas and material
To attend trade meetings and industry conventions
To cultivate effective business relationships with executive decision makers in key accounts

Education and Experience:
Business degree or related professional qualification

---

1. Based on http://www.best-job-interview.com/sales-manager-job-description.html.

Experience in all aspects of planning and implementing sales strategy
Technical sales 7._____
Proven experience in customer 8._____ management
Knowledge of market research
Experience in managing and directing a sales team
Relevant product and industry knowledge
Experience with relevant software applications
Key Competencies:
Excellent written and verbal 9._____ skills
Organization and planning
Problem analysis and problem-solving
Information management
Team-leadership
Formal 10._____ skills
Persuasiveness
Adaptability
Innovation
Judgment
Decision-making
Stress tolerance

1. A. movements   B. events   C. activities
2. A. subjectives B. objectives   C. aims
3. A. achievement B. satisfaction   C. happiness
4. A. performance B. degree   C. ability
5. A. weekly   B. quarterly   C. yearly
6. A. profit   B. interest   C. expenses
7. A. technology   B. skills   C. abilities
8. A. relationship B. friendship   C. complain
9. A. exchange   B. discussion   C. communication
10. A. talking   B. presentation   C. telling

Writing: Application Letter

Write an application letter with the following information.
- Applying for the job as sales representative advertised in China Daily on February 26th, 2013.
- Education (Shenzhen Business School) and Experience (Huashan Groups for two years).
- Enclosed CV
- Contact: 136-8973-6543
- (100-150 words)

SHENZHEN POLYTECHNIC
No. 4089, West Shahe Road
Xili Lake
Nanshan District
Shenzhen 518055
China

Feb. 26th, 2013

HR Department
Shenzhen Nanshan Textiles import and Export Corp.
2045 Nanshan Avenue
Nanshan District
Shenzhen 518052
China

Gentlemen:

Yours sincerely,
Wang Xiaohua
Wang Xiaohua

Encl: CV

Module Two
Interviewing for an International Business Job

导入案例

　　工作面试性格测试。

任务要求

　　学生分成三人一组，分别扮演应聘者、招聘公司人力资源部经理，招聘岗位所在部门经理，完成面试通知及回复、面试、录用通知和任命通知等任务。

任务流程

1. 人力资源部经理用传真通知应聘者进行面试。
2. 应聘者收到面试通知后，向人力资源部经理回复电子邮件表示感谢。
3. 人力资源部经理和进出口部经理作为面试官，对应聘者进行面试。
4. 人力资源部经理向应聘者发出录用通知。
5. 职位所在部门经理发任命通知给该部门全体员工。

知识要点

1. 国际商务沟通。
2. 内部沟通和外部沟通。
3. 商务沟通流向。
4. 商务沟通渠道。

技能要求

1. 词汇：工作类别。
2. 听：面试。
3. 说：面试礼仪。
4. 读：新浪声称占领中国微博市场。
5. 写：面试感谢信。

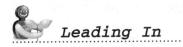 Leading In

Job Interview Personality Test [1]

You are being interviewed for a new job.

For each of the following questions try to find the skills or qualities that the interviewer is most likely looking for.

1. You are asked to talk about a problem that you solved in a unique way. The interviewer wants to know more about your

　　A. Creativity skills

　　B. Persuasion skills

　　C. Communication skills

　　D. Organizational skills

　　E. Intelligence

2. You are asked to talk about a time when you had to choose between two equally attractive options. The interviewer wants to know more about your

　　A. Problem solving skills

　　B. Persuasion skills

　　C. Leadership skills

　　D. Communication skills

　　E. Creativity

3. You are asked to comment about an occasion where you had to convince someone to see things your way. The interviewer wants to know more about your

　　A. Organizational skills

　　B. Communication skills

　　C. Problem solving skills

　　D. Motivation

　　E. Time management skills

4. You are asked to talk about a time where you had to make an extraordinary effort in order to fulfill a deadline. The interviewer wants to know more about your

　　A. Motivation

　　B. Decision making skills

　　C. Leadership skills

　　D. Persuasion skills

　　E. Creativity

---

1. Based on http://www.personalitytest.net/quizzes/quiz4/index.htm.

5. You are asked to talk about any academic courses or degrees that you dropped or left uncompleted. The interviewer wants to know more about your

A. Self-confidence

B. Perseverance

C. Integrity

D. Loyalty

E. Education

6. You are asked to talk about a time when you had to resolve any conflicts that arose from managing a team. The interviewer wants to know more about your

A. Multi-tasking skills

B. Initiative

C. Leadership skills

D. Persuasion skills

E. Motivation

7. You are asked to talk about a time when you presented a case in order to influence someone's opinion. The interviewer wants to know more about your

A. Creativity skills

B. Motivation

C. Initiative

D. Organizational skills

E. Intelligence

 Task Requirements

The students are divided into groups with 3 members each. Student A plays a role as an applicant. Student B plays a role as the HR manager. And student C plays a role as the manager of the department for which the applicant is applying. They will finish the tasks together as follows.

Task 1 Writing an Interview Notice by Fax

A fax (short for facsimile) is the telephonic transmission of scanned-in printed material (text or images), usually to a telephone number associated with a printer or other output device. Fax is a formal method to send notice which contains letter head, fax information, salutation, the body of the fax, complimentary close and signature.

Student B plays a role as Bridges Thompson, the HR manager of Rainbow Pet Products Co., Ltd., Los Angeles, California.

After receiving the memo from Christine Winters, he sends a formal interview notice to Daniel Zheng by fax on Sept. 25th, 2012.

Write a fax with the following information.

- Express thanks for applying for the job
- The reason for interviewing
- The venue, date and time of the interview (at 9 a.m. on Oct. 5th, 2012 in room 203)
- Requirements for any changes

(50-100 words)

Rainbow Pet Products Co., Ltd., Los Angeles, California.
1358 Westwood Blvd, Los Angeles, CA90024-4911, USA
Tel:
Fax:
E-mail:

FAX MESSAGE
To:
Fax Number:
From:
Date:
Number of Pages (including this page): 1

Dear Mr. Zheng:

Hereby notified.

Sincerely Yours,
Rainbow Pet Products Co., Ltd., Los Angeles, California
Bridges Thompson
Bridges Thompson
HR Manager

Task 2 Writing a Thank-you Letter by E-mail

Electronic mail, also known as email or e-mail, is a method of exchanging digital messages from an author to one or more recipients. Modern email operates across the internet or other computer networks. E-mail is much less formal than a written letter. E-mails are usually short and concise. When writing to someone you know well, feel free to write as if you are speaking to the person. Abbreviated verb forms are often used in e-mail.

Student A plays a role as Daniel Zheng. After receiving the notice of the interview, he takes a few minutes to express his appreciation by e-mail on Sept. 26th, 2012.

 Write an e-mail including the following information.
- Express thanks for the interview notice
- Be specific about which is appreciated
- Promise to be on time
- End with a positive statement

(50-100 words)

| From: |
| Date: |
| To: |
| Cc: |
| Subject: |
| |

Task 3 Having an Interview

Interview is a somewhat formal discussion between a hirer and an applicant or candidate, typically in person, in which information is exchanged, with the intention of establishing the applicant's suitability for a position. It should be a two-way process.

Make sure that you are well prepared before the interview. Think about what kind of questions you might be asked and how you should answer them. Make a note of the questions you want to ask and take them into the interview with you.

Make sure to be on time and look presentable. The first impression counts. You don't get a second chance to make a first impression—make sure it is a good one.

Make sure you know exactly what the job vacancy requires—not only the qualifications and experience, but also the essential qualities such as commitment, initiative, willingness to learn, creativities and communication skills.

Here are some questions to help you.
- What does the company do?
- What's involved in the position you're applying for?
- What qualifications do you need for the position?
- What kind of skills is the employer looking for?
- Who are the customers or clients?
- What kind of reputation does the employer have?

If you want to be successful in interview, you should not only know something about the company you are applying for, but also know yourself. Having knowledge about your skills, abilities, personal qualities, values and interests alongside an understanding of what you want from a job or career can provide you with a sense of direction and purpose that is crucial in any job search. Be sure to know yourself better.
- Why do you want this job?
- How did you become interested in this field of work?
- What do you have to offer this company?
- What are some of your strengths and weaknesses?
- What do you see yourself doing in the future?

Student A plays a role as Daniel Zheng. He takes part in the interview at 9 a.m. on Oct. 5th, 2012 in room 203.

Student B plays a role as Bridges Thompson, the HR manager of Rainbow Pet Products Co., Ltd., Los Angeles, California.

Student C plays a role as Christine Winters, the international sales manager of Rainbow Pet Products Co., Ltd., Los Angeles, California.

Bridges Thompson and Christine Winters are all interviewers. They ask at least 10 questions to Daniel Zheng. And Daniel Zheng asks at least 2 questions.

Simulate the interview according to the above information.

Task 4 Making a Job Offer

A job offer is an invitation for a potential employee to become an employee in the organization. The job offer contains the details of employment offer.

The initial job offer may be extended verbally, but most employers follow up with a written job offer that may take the form of a job offer letter or an employment contract.

A job offer typically contains the salary offered for the job, standard employee benefits, the job title of the position, the name of the supervisor of the position, and other terms and conditions of employment.

Student A plays a role as Daniel Zheng.

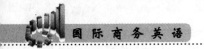

Student B plays a role as Bridges Thompson, the HR manager of Rainbow Pet Products Co., Ltd., Los Angeles, California.

After discussing with Christine Winters, the manager of the International Sales of Rainbow Pet Products Co., Ltd., Los Angeles, Bridges Thompson sends Daniel Zheng a job offer on Oct. 10th, 2012 that they have decided to recruit Daniel Zheng as the international salesperson in the International Sales Department.

Please fill in the following Job Offer written by Bridges Thompson and accepted by Daniel Zheng.

a. Date
b. Employee's Name and Address
c. Employee's Name
d. Title of Position
e. Department and Company Name
f. Permanent or Temporary
g. Name of the Manager of the Department which provided the Job
h. Start Date: Nov. 1st, 2012
i. Job Responsibilities
j. Compensation
k. Holidays and Vocations
l. Due Date: Oct. 30th, 2012
m. Name of HR Manager
n. Date of Signature: Oct. 25th, 2012
o. Signature of the Employee
p. Contact of the Company

---

a. _____

b. _____
_____
_____

Dear c. _____ :

Re: Employment with d. _____, e. _____

I am very pleased to offer you a f. _____ position as d. _____, e. _____ based on the following terms and conditions:

Position: d. _____

Module Two *Interviewing for an International Business Job*

You are appointed to the position of d._____, e._____, and in this capacity, you will report directly to g._____. This is a f._____ position, and as discussed and agreed with you, your start date in the position will be h._____.

In this assignment of d._____, your key responsibilities will be as the follows i._____.
   _____.
   _____.
   _____.
   _____.

Remuneration:

Your base salary j._____. Your salary is payable once a month on the 7th day every month.

Your hours of work are based on the normal operating hours of the Company and are expected to be from 9:00 a.m. to 5:00 p.m., Monday to Friday, with a one hour lunch break, amounting to 35 hours per week.

Benefits and Pension:

Please refer to the Human Resources website for Benefits and Pension information specific to your appointment.

Vacation:

You will receive k._____ per year.

5. Professional Allowance:

Assessment Period:

We will review your progress in the position on a regular basis and provide you with regular feedback.

Effective Date:

The terms of this offer shall come into effect on your first day of employment.

I would ask that you review the contents of this offer carefully. If the terms of employment as set out in this agreement are acceptable to you, please sign and date one copy and return a fully signed copy to my attention by l._____.

c._____, I wish to convey my sincere enthusiasm about the possibility of you joining the d._____, e._____. I hope that you find the terms of this offer reasonable and attractive.

Please feel free to contact me if you have any questions.

Yours truly,

m._____ HR Manager
I agree to accept the conditions of employment indicated above, n._____. o._____ NOTE: Please ensure that you forward a copy of the accepted letter l._____: p._____ _____ _____ _____

Task 5 Sending an Appointment Notice by Memo

An appointment notice is a notice to tell all of the staff in a company or a department that someone has been one of the members of the company and his specific position.

Student C plays a role as Christine Winters, the International Sales Manager of Rainbow Pet Products Co., Ltd., Los Angeles, California.

She sends a Memo to all the staff of the international sales department to announce the appointment of Daniel Zheng as the international salesperson on Nov. 1st, 2012.

 Fill in the blanks in the memorandum according to the above information.

MEMO To: From: Date: Subject:
Research by _____ and _____, the new appointed relevant personnel as follows: Appoint _____ as Salesperson in _____. The above appointments decided on the date of issuance that is beginning to be implemented. Hereby appoint.

Module Two *Interviewing for an International Business Job*

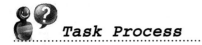

Task 1   Writing an Interview Notice

Rainbow Pet Products Co., Ltd., Los Angeles, California.
1358 Westwood Blvd, Los Angeles, CA90024-4911, USA
Tel: 213-345-9109
Fax: 213-345-9108
E-mail: bridgesthompson@yahoo.com

FAX MESSAGE
To: Daniel Zheng
Fax Number: 318-861-2119
From: Bridges Thompson, Manager of HR Department
Date: Sept. 25th, 2012
Number of Pages (including this page): 1

Dear Mr. Zheng:

Thank you for applying for a job in our company.

Your knowledge and experiences gave us a good impression. In order to further our understanding of each other, please come to our company at 9 a.m. on Oct. 5th, 2012 in room 203 in our company to take part in the interview.

If it is not convenient for you please contact me beforehand.

Hereby notified.

Sincerely Yours,
Rainbow Pet Products Co., Ltd., Los Angeles, California
Bridges Thompson
Bridges Thompson
HR Manager

Task 2 Writing a Thank-you Letter by E-mail

From: danielzheng@yahoo.com
Date: Sept. 26th, 2012
To: bridgesthompson@yahoo.com
Cc:
Subject: Interview
Mr. Thompson Thank you for your fax of Sept. 25th, 2012. I'm glad to have the opportunity of the interview. It is my pleasure to have the chance to be a salesperson for your company. I'll be there on time. I'm looking forward to the interview. Best Regards Daniel Zheng

Task 3 Having an Interview

Daniel Zheng: Good morning. My name is Daniel Zheng. Here's my CV. It's my pleasure to have the opportunity for the interview.

Bridges Thompson: Good morning, Daniel. I'm Bridges Thompson, the HR manager. This is Christine Winters, the manager of International Sales Department.

Christine Winters: Nice to meet you, Daniel.

Daniel Zheng: Nice to meet you, Mrs. Winters.

Bridges Thompson: Please take a seat.

Daniel Zheng: Thank you, Mr. Thompson.

Bridges Thompson: OK, Daniel. We've seen your Résumé and would you like to tell me a little about yourself?

Daniel Zheng: Of course. I'm 24 years old. I come from China. After I graduated from high school, I furthered my study in American Commercial College. My major is International Business. For the past two years, I have worked as a salesperson for Cool Ice-cream House. I learned from your job advertisement that you are going to explore Asian markets. China is one of

Module Two *Interviewing for an International Business Job*

the biggest markets in the world. My Chinese background and my excellent communication skills both in Chinese and in English would be a definite asset for your company.

Christine Winters: We learned from your Résumé, you have been awarded as the Employee of the 2011 Award in Cool Ice-cream House. Since you have been good in your last job, why did you leave?

Daniel Zheng: I love that job. But as you know, I majored in international Business. The Cool Ice-cream House is a local enterprise dealing with domestic business. I'm eager to take the advantages of my study in the college. I have talked with Mr. Hughes, my boss in Cool Ice-cream house, and he supports my decision. And he would like to write a recommendation letter for me, if you need it.

Bridges Thompson: What do you know about our company?

Daniel Zheng: Rainbow Pet Products Co., Ltd. is specialized in Pet Products in USA. You are one of the leading companies in selling Pets Products. And you are going to explore Asian market at present.

Christine Winters: Why do you want to work for us?

Daniel Zheng: When I saw your job advertisement on the Internet, I believe it is a good chance for me. I'm Chinese, and I have the advantages to communicate with Chinese. With the great development of Chinese economy, I don't want to miss the chance to further my career in international business between USA and China.

Bridges Thompson: What're your great strengths?

Daniel Zheng: My Chinese background maybe the greatest strengths for the position in your company. And I also have the knowledge of principles and practices of sales, and I am skilled in organizing meetings, making presentations, writing reports and dealing with customers. I can thrive under pressure. I'm a great motivator, and an amazing problem solver.

Bridges Thompson: What's your biggest weakness?

Daniel Zheng: I've been told I occasionally focus on details and miss the bigger picture, so I've been spending time laying out the complete project every day to see my overall progress.

Christine Winters: What do you know about the position you are applying for?

Daniel Zheng: As an international salesperson, I should be responsible for planning and carrying out international sales activities, ensuring customer satisfaction, managing quality of product and service delivery.

Christine Winters: Do you think that your experience can support you to fill the job?

Nicole: I do have the confidence to carry out the task with my full effort. I feel I would be especially qualified to work in this position because of my interest and experience in sales and marketing.

Christine Winters: What would you like to do once you get the job?

Daniel Zheng: Firstly, I'd like to make an international market research and develop a customer database and prepare promotional materials. And then I'd like to make international sales calls or send promotion letters to potential clients. If there are any responds and concerns

by phone, electronically or in person, I'd like to negotiate with them in order to sign a win-win contract. After that, I will try my best to ensure customer service satisfaction and good client relationships by following up on international sales activity and service delivery.

Christine Winters: Are you good at working in a team?

Daniel Zheng: Of course. I believe there's a lot of teamwork in sales especially international sales. No one works in a vacuum. When people come together and work together, teamwork spirit encourages creativity, and gives the team a shared experience.

Bridges Thompson: Do you have any questions to ask us?

Daniel Zheng: Yes. The basic salary is OK for me. But I really want to know the commission rate.

Bridges Thompson: The commission rate is 3% for the first three months. And after three months, you can earn 5% commission. If you have the chance to promote, not only the basic salary, but also the commission will be raised.

Daniel Zheng: How soon could I start, if I were offered the job?

Bridges Thompson: You will receive the offer in a week if you get the job. And you can start your job at the beginning of the next month. How should I tell you about our final decision?

Daniel Zheng: I can be reached at any time by mobile phone. I expect to hear from you as early as possible.

Bridges Thompson: We'll contact you by the end of this week. Thank you for your coming. Hope to see you again.

Daniel Zheng: Thank you very much. Good-bye.

Task 4 Making a Job Offer

Oct. 10th, 2012

Daniel Zheng
3014 Knight St. Shreveport, LA 71105, USA
Tel: 866-8736-5632
Fax: 318-861-2119
E-mail: danielzheng@yahoo.com.

Dear Daniel Zheng:

Re: Employment with International Salesperson, International Sales Department, Rainbow Pet Products Co., Ltd., Los Angeles, California

I am very pleased to offer you a permanent position as International Salesperson, International Sales Department, Rainbow Pet Products Co., Ltd., Los Angeles, California based on the following terms and conditions:

Module Two *Interviewing for an International Business Job*

Position: <u>International Salesperson</u>

You are appointed to the position of <u>International Salesperson, International Sales Department, Rainbow Pet Products Co., Ltd., Los Angeles, California,</u> and in this capacity, you will report directly to <u>Christine Winters</u>. This is a <u>permanent</u> position, and as discussed and agreed with you, your start date in the position will be <u>Nov. 1st, 2012.</u>

In this assignment of <u>international salesperson</u>, your key responsibilities will be <u>as the following</u>:
<u>To make international market research and surveys</u>
<u>To develop and maintain a customer database and promotional materials</u>
<u>To schedule and conduct international sales and marketing activity</u>
<u>To make international sales calls to new or existing clients</u>
<u>To develop and make presentations of company products and services to current and potential clients</u>
<u>To respond to international sales inquiries and concerns by phone, electronically or in person</u>
<u>To negotiate with international clients</u>
<u>To fulfill international sales contracts</u>
<u>To ensure customer service satisfaction and good client relationships</u>
<u>To follow up on international sales activity and service delivery</u>
<u>To perform quality checks on product</u>
<u>To maintain international sales activity records and prepare sales reports</u>

Remuneration:

Your base salary <u>USD 1.5k each month plus 3% commission for the first three months and after that USD 1.5k each month plus 5% commission.</u> Your salary is payable once a month on the 7th day every week.

Your hours of work are based on the normal operating hours of the Company and are expected to be from 9:00 a.m. to 5:00 p.m., Monday to Friday, with a one-hour lunch break, amounting to 35 hours per week.

Benefits and Pension:

Please refer to the Human Resources website for Benefits and Pension information specific to your appointment.

Vacation:

You will receive <u>2-week vacation and 10 days paid holidays</u> per year.

5. Professional Allowance:

Assessment Period:

We will review your progress in the position on a regular basis and provide you with regular feedback.

Effective Date:

The terms of this offer shall come into effect on your first day of employment.

I would ask that you review the contents of this offer carefully. If the terms of employment as set out in this agreement are acceptable to you, please sign and date one copy and return a fully signed copy to my attention by Oct. 30th, 2012.

Daniel Zheng: I wish to convey my sincere enthusiasm about the possibility of you joining the International Salesperson, International Sales Department, Rainbow Pet Products Co., Ltd., Los Angeles, California. I hope that you find the terms of this offer reasonable and attractive.

Please feel free to contact me if you have any questions.

Yours truly,
Bridges Thompson
HR Manager

I agree to accept the conditions of employment indicated above, Oct. 25th, 2012   .

Daniel Zheng

NOTE: Please ensure that you forward a copy of the accepted letter before Oct. 30th, 2012   :

HR department
Rainbow Pet Products Co., Ltd., Los Angeles, California.
1358 Westwood Blvd, Los Angeles, CA90024-4911
Tel: 213-345-9109
Fax: 213-345-9108
E-mail: bridgesthompson@yahoo.com

Task 5 Sending an Appointment Notice by Memo

MEMO
To All of the Staff in International Sales Department
From Christine Winters, International Sales Manager
Date Nov. 1st, 2012
Subject Appointment

Research by International Sales Department and HR Department the new appointed relevant personnel as follows: Appoint Daniel Zheng as Salesperson in International Sales Department.

The above appointments decided on the date of issuance that is beginning to be implemented.

Hereby appoint.

Module Two *Interviewing for an International Business Job*

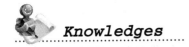

International Business Communication

Communication is the exchange of thoughts, messages, or information, by speech, signals, writing, or behaviour between a sender and a receiver. There are eight factors in communication. They are sender, receiver, message (idea-reception-understanding), encode, decode, medium, feedback, noise and context.

Sender is the participant in the communication process who communicate messages to an audience.

A message is the written, oral, or nonverbal information that sender transmits to an audience.

Receiver is the audience to whom messages are directed.

Encoding is the process of selecting words and their order for a message by a sender.

Decoding is translation of a message by a receiver.

Medium is the conduit or Message channel that will carry a message from the sender to the receiver.

Noise, literally or figuratively, is anything that interferes with a message.

Feedback is a verbal or nonverbal response by a receiver to the sender's.

Context refers to the situation in which communication takes place and every factor affecting its transmission.

International Communication is the ability to speak and write in ways that are sensitive to and cognizant of the factors in different cultural contexts.

International Business Communication is defined as the communications within and between businesses that involve people from more than one nation or region.

Practice: Tell the process of communication according to chart 2-1 in your own words.

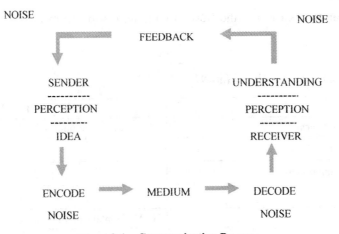

Chart 2-1 Communication Process

Internal Communication and External Communication

Internal communication involves communicating back and forth within the organization among employees and owners through such written and oral channels as memos, reports, proposals, meetings, oral presentations, speeches, and person-to-person and telephone conversations.

External communication refers to communication with an organization's major audiences, the general public, customers, vendors and other businesses, and government officials.

Practice: Match column I with column II.

I	II
1. Press Release	A. Internal Communication
2. Team building	
3. Client reception	
4. Regular meeting	
5. Marketing Research	B. External Communication
6. Public Relation	
7. Tax Declare	
8. Department cooperation	

The Flow of Communication

Communication can flow in several directions.

Downward communication is the flow of communication from upper management to middle management or lower management.

Horizontal communication is the flow of communication moving laterally or at the same level in the organization.

Upward communication is the flow of communication from lower managers to upper managers.

Practice: Match column I with column II.

I	II
1. Management directives	A. Upward Communication
2. Job plans, policies	
3. Suggestions for improvement	
4. Conflict resolution	
5. Mission statements	B. Horizontal Communication
6. Task coordination	

Module Two Interviewing for an International Business Job

7. Information sharing	
8. Problem solving	
9. Anonymous hotline	C. Downward Communication
10. Employee feedback	
11. Company goals	
12. Progress reports	
13. Reports of customer interaction, feedback	

The Channel of Communication

The Channel of communication are as follows (Table 2-1).

Table 2-1 Communication Channel

	Written	Oral
Traditional	Memo Letter (Surface mail) Plan Report Company Newsletter Bulletin board Posting Orientation manual	Face-to-face Company Meetings Team Meetings Conference Press Release Presentation Speech
Electronic	E-mail Fax Telegram Telex Instant Messaging BBS(Bulletin Board System) Blog My Space Msn & QQ Mass Storage Device Twitter Microblog	Telephone Cell Phone Voicemail Video Conferencing

Practice: Selecting the best channel from Table 2-1.

_____1. To share personal message, be persuasive, or deliver bad news; richest communication channel.

_____2. For convenience when nonverbal cues are unimportant.

_____3. To leave message for response when convenient

_____4. To cross time zones, to produce written record, for speedy delivery
_____5. When group decisions and consensus are important
_____6. To disperse data or elicit consensus from geographically dispersed group
_____7. To produce formal, written record for insiders
_____8. To produce formal, written record for customers and other outsiders
_____9. To deliver complex data internally or externally

Skills Requirements

Vocabulary: Work Categories

List as much jobs as you can in the table according to the work categories they belong to.

Category	Jobs
Administrative	
Business	
Construction	
Education	
Engineering	
Health	
Hospitality	
Legal	
Maintenance	
Manufacturing	
Media	
Sales	
Technology	
Transportation	
Agriculture	

Module Two *Interviewing for an International Business Job*

Listening: Interview

 Listen to the dialogues twice, and choose the best answer.

1. Which one is not mentioned in the interview?
   A. Hardworking   B. Goal-driven
   C. Responsible   D. Persuasive
2. How many years has the interviewee been working as a computer programmer?
   A. 2 years   B. 3 years
   C. 4 years   D. 5 years
3. Why did the interviewee leave his last job?
   A. Low Salary   B. Without Promotion Chance
   C. Bad Interpersonal Relationship   D. All of the above
4. What kind of person is Mr. Chen?
   A. Honest   B. Responsible
   C. Hardworking   D. All of the above
5. How many projects has the interviewee finished?
   A. 1   B. 2
   C. 3   D. 4

Speaking: Interview Etiquette

Work in pairs with a partner. Look at the question. Take one minute to prepare your answer. Think of reasons to explain your choice. Then tell your partner your answer and reasons.

WHAT IS IMPORTANT WHEN …?
Having an interview

- Dress for success
- Time keeping
- Be honest

41

Reading: Sina Claims Lead in China's Micro-blog Market

 Read the article below. Choose the best answer (A, B or C).

Sina Claims Lead in China's Micro-blog Market [1]

BEIJING, Nov. 16, 2010 (Xinhua) — Internet portal Sina.com Tuesday claimed victory in battle for China's micro-blog market, announcing it has 50 million registered users of its Twitter-like service after 14 months of operation.

Sina launched its Chinese-language micro-blogging service on Aug. 28 last year and had attracted 10 million users by April.

The company claimed its "absolute leading position" in China's Micro-Blog business in a statement issued on Tuesday, although competitors such as Netease, Sohu and Tencent have not revealed their micro-blog user numbers.

All the providers of accessible Micro-Blogging services in China are domestic companies.

China has the world's largest number of Internet users at about 400 million.

Allowing users to post pictures and video clips with up to 140 Chinese characters, Sina's micro-blogging service has become a major channel of breaking news items on the Internet.

"One of the major advantages compared with other products is that Sina's Micro-Blogging is more compatible with mobile devices," said Sina vice president Peng Shaobin at a press conference in Beijing.

According to Sina's statistics, about 38 percent of new information every day is posted through Internet-connected mobile terminals. The proportion would increase with the development of third-generation telecommunications, said Peng.

---

1. Sina Micro-Blog launched in 2008.
   A. True   B. False   C. Not mentioned

2. Tencent is one of Sina Micro-Blog's competitors.
   A. True   B. False   C. Not mentioned

3. Easy is one of the major advantages of Micro-Blog.
   A. True   B. False   C. Not mentioned

4. Micro-Blogging services is absolutely the same as twitter.
   A. True   B. False   C. Not mentioned

5. There are only 400 million internet users in China.
   A. True   B. False   C. Not mentioned

---

1. Based on http://english.sina.com/technology/2010/1116/348289.html.

Module Two *Interviewing for an International Business Job*

Writing: Thank-you Email after an Interview

 Write a Thank-you E-mail after an interview.
- Express thanks for the interview
- Self promotion
- Enclosed reference

(100-150 words)

From: emilybrown@yahoo.com
Date: Sept. 26, 2012
To: abccoltd@yahoo.com
Cc:
Subject: Interview
Mr. Lee   Best Regards Emily Brown

Module Three
Working Environment

导入案例
　　你有创业的条件吗？

任务要求
　　学生分成五人一组，分别扮演新员工、老员工、公司部门经理及秘书，用英文完成员工入职第一天的工作任务。

任务流程
　1. 新员工第一天上班向部门经理报道。
　2. 部门秘书向新员工介绍工作环境及办公设备的使用方法。
　3. 给新员工设计名片和门卡。

知识要点
　1. 国际商务宏观环境。
　2. 国际商务微观环境。

技能要求
　1. 词汇：办公设施。
　2. 听：问路。
　3. 说：第一天上班注意事项。
　4. 读：开始一份新工作。
　5. 写：便条。

Module Three   *Working Environment*

 *Leading In*

Should You Be an Entrepreneur? [1]

Studies of successful entrepreneurs reveal common characteristics—family backgrounds, experiences, motivations, personality traits, behaviors, values, and beliefs. How do you fit these patterns? What is your E.Q. (Entrepreneurial Quotient)? Northwestern Mutual Life has created the following test to predict how suited you are to entrepreneurship. This test cannot predict your success—it can only give you an idea whether you will have a head start or a handicap with which to work. Entrepreneurial skills can be learned. The test is intended to help you see how you compare with others who have been successful entrepreneurs.

Add or subtract your score as you evaluate yourself:

Significantly high numbers of entrepreneurs are children of first-generation Americans. If your parents immigrated to the United States, score one. If not, score minus one.

Successful entrepreneurs are not, as a rule, top achievers in school. If you were a top student, subtract four. If not, add four.

Entrepreneurs are not especially enthusiastic about participating in group activities in school. If you enjoyed group activities—clubs, team sports, double dates—subtract one. If not, add one.

Studies of entrepreneurs show that, as youngsters, they often preferred to be alone. Did you prefer to be alone as a youngster? If so, add one. If not, subtract one.

Those who started enterprises during childhood—lemonade stands, family newspapers, greeting card sales—or ran for elected office at school can add two, because enterprise usually can be traced to an early age. If you didn't initiate enterprises, subtract two.

Stubbornness as a child seems to translate into determination to do things one's own way—a hallmark of proven entrepreneurs. If you were stubborn as a child, add one. If not, subtract one.

Caution may involve an unwillingness to take risks, a handicap for those embarking on previously uncharted territory. Were you a cautious youngster? If yes, deduct four. If no, add four.

If you were daring or adventuresome, add four more.

Entrepreneurs often have the faith to pursue different paths despite the opinions of others. If the opinions of others matter a lot to you, subtract one. If not, add one.

Being tired of a daily routine often precipitates an entrepreneur's decision to start an enterprise. If changing your daily routine would be an important motivation for starting your own enterprise, add two. If not, subtract two.

Yes, you really enjoy work. But are you willing to work overnight? If yes, add two. If no, subtract two.

---

1. Based on http://dosen.narotama.ac.id.

If you are willing to work as long as it takes with little or no sleep to finish a job, add four more.

Entrepreneurs generally enjoy their type of work so much they move from one project to another—non-stop. When you complete a project successfully, do you immediately start another? If yes, add two. If no, subtract two.

Successful entrepreneurs are willing to use their savings to finance a project. If you are willing to commit your savings to start a business, add two. If not, subtract two.

Would you be willing to borrow from others? Then add two more. If not, subtract two.

If your business should fail, would you immediately start working on another? If yes, add four. If no, subtract four.

Or, if you would immediately start looking for a job with a regular paycheck, subtract one more.

Do you believe being an entrepreneur is risky? If yes, subtract two. If no, add two.

Many entrepreneurs put their long-term and short-term goals in writing. If you do, add one. If you don't, subtract one.

Handling cash flow can be critical to entrepreneurial success. Do you believe you have the ability to deal with cash flow in a professional manner? If so, add two. If not, subtract two.

Entrepreneurial personalities seems to be easily bored. If you are easily bored, add two. If not, subtract two.

Optimism can fuel the drive to press for success in uncharted waters. If you're an optimist, add two. Pessimist, subtract two.

 *Task Requirements*

The students are divided into groups with 5 members each. Student A plays a role as the new staff. Student B plays a role as the secretary of the International Sales Department. Student C plays a role as the manager of International Sales Department. Student D and E play the roles as the coworkers in the department. They will finish the tasks together as follows.

Task 1　Reporting for the First Day of Work

On your first day of work, it is necessary for you to report directly to the manager of the department. From navigating your first day of work, you'd better collect necessary information beforehand so that you can be comfortable and prepared as you begin working. Please refer to your offer letter for the exact location of your orientation and the necessary document needed.

Student A plays a role as Daniel Zheng, the new international salesperson of the International Sales Department of Rainbow Pet Products Co., Ltd., Los Angeles, California.

Student B plays a role as Ella Finger, the secretary of the International Sales Department of Rainbow Pet Products Co., Ltd., Los Angeles, California.

Student C plays a role as Christine Winters, the manager of the International Sales Department of Rainbow Pet Products Co., Ltd., Los Angeles, California.

Module Three Working Environment

Student D plays a role as Andrew Hard, the director of the Asian section of International Sales Department of Rainbow Pet Products Co., Ltd., Los Angeles, California.. Student E plays a role as Amelia Hill, the international salesperson in the Asian section of the International Sales Department of Rainbow Pet Products Co., Ltd., Los Angeles, California.

Daniel Zheng reports for the first day of work at 9 a.m. on Nov. 1st, 2012. Ella Finger greets Daniel Zheng and calls Christine Winters to ask whether she has time to meet Daniel Zheng. And then shows Daniel Zheng into the manager's office. Christine Winters welcomes Daniel Zheng into her sales team. And she makes a brief introduction of the International Sales Department and encourages Daniel Zheng to do a good job. Then she introduces Daniel to the other members in the Asian section office. Andrew Hard and Amelia Hill greet Daniel Zheng. Ella Finger comes in and reminds Christine Winters that she has an appointment with Mr. White. And then Ella Finger shows Daniel Zheng around instead of Christine Winters.

 Simulate the situation according to the above information.

Task 2 Being Familiar with Work Environment

A work environment can be identified as the place that one works, such as the traffic situation, office building, office room, office furniture, office equipment, office stationary. We tend, however, to hear about "healthy work environments." This can point to other factors in the work environment, such as co-workers, management, health care, company culture and so on.

Student A plays a role as Daniel Zheng, the new international salesperson of the International Sales Department of Rainbow Pet Products Co., Ltd., Los Angeles, California.

Student B plays a role as Ella Finger, the secretary of the International Sales Department of Rainbow Pet Products Co., Ltd., Los Angeles, California.

Ella Finger tells Daniel Zheng where his cubicle is. She gives him a pile of files for the new comer, such as company brochure, product catalogue, job description, employee handbook, client information. She tells Daniel his telephone number (213-345-9125), his computer password (IS9837-3656). She also tells him where to apply for office stationary and where to borrow office equipment (in the back office). And then she shows Daniel Zheng around. She tells him the layout of the company according to Table 3-1 and Chart 3-1. And then shows him how to use the fax machine. After that she tells Daniel the work hour (9:00 a.m. to 5:00 p.m. with one hour for lunch at 11:30 a.m.) and the payday (the 7th every month). At last she asks him to call the back office (213-345-9118) about designing the business card and ID badge.

Table 3-1 Layout of the Company

The top floor	Administrative and Financial Department	CEO's office	HR Department
The third floor	International Sales Department	Back Office	Domestic Sales Department
		Rest Room	
The second floor	R&D Department	Conference Room	Customer Service Department
The first floor	Product Department	Conference Room	Logistic Department

The Third Floor

International Sales Asian Section Office	Back Office	Domestic Sales East Section Office
International Sales Manager's Office	Rest Room	Domestic Sales Manager's Office
International Sales European Section Office		Domestic Sales West Section Office

Chart 3-1 Layout of the Third Floor

 Simulate the situation according to the above information.

Task 3 Designing Business Card and ID Badge

Business Cards are cards bearing business information about a company or individual. They are shared during formal introductions as a convenience and a memory aid. A business card typically includes the giver's name, company affiliation (usually with a logo) and contact information such as street addresses, telephone number, fax number, e-mail addresses or website. Traditionally many cards were simple black text on white stock; today a professional business card will sometimes include one or more aspects of striking visual design.

Business cards are printed on some form of card stock, the visual effect, method of printing, cost and other details varying according to cultural or organizational norms and personal preferences.

ID badges are easy to use and convenient for employees, and authorized visitors. ID badges integrate transparently with existing security and access control systems and provide a high level of confidence and security for the workplace. An ID badge often contains the following information: logo, company's name, department, position, employee's number, employee's name,

Module Three Working Environment

employee's signature, and employee's photo.

Student A plays a role as Daniel Zheng, the new international salesperson in the International Sales Department of Rainbow Pet Products Co., Ltd., Los Angeles, California. His employee number is IS9837-3656. He designs the Business Card and ID Badge after Ella telling him to do so.

Address: 1358 Westwood Blvd, Los Angeles, CA90024-4911, USA

Tel: 213-345-9125

Fax: 213-345-9125

E-mail:danielzheng@yahoo.com

 Design the Card with the following information.
- Name
- Position, Department
- Address
- Telephone Number
- Fax
- E-mail Address

Rainbow Pet Products Corp., Los Angeles, California

 Design the ID Badge with the following information.
- Employee's Name
- Department
- Position
- Employee's Number
- Employee's Signature

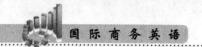

Task Process

Task 1 Reporting for the First Day of Work

Ella Finger: Good morning. May I help you?

Daniel Zheng: Good morning, my name is Daniel Zheng. I'm reporting for work as an international salesperson today.

Ella Finger: Nice to meet you, Mr. Zheng. I'm Ella Finger, the secretary of International Sales Department. Wait a minute, please.

(Ella Finger calls Mrs. Winters on the phone)

Ella Finger: Mrs. Winters, Mr. Zheng is here. Would you like to see him now?

Christine Winters: Yeah, Let him in.

(Ella Finger hangs up.)

Ella Finger: Mr. Zheng, she's ready for you. Come this way.

Module Three Working Environment

Daniel Zheng: Thank you.

(Ella Finger knocks at the door.)

Christine Winters: Come in, come in.

(Ella Finger opens the door, and lets Daniel Zheng in, and then closes the door.)

Daniel Zheng: Good Morning, Mrs. Winters. I'm Daniel Zheng. I'm here to report for work.

Christine Winters: Daniel, welcome to our International Sales Department. Take a seat please.

Daniel Zheng: Thank you.

Christine Winters: I'm happy to have you as part of the talented, dedicated team. Have you talked with Mr. Thompson?

Daniel Zheng: Yes, I have talked with him and learned the basic company policies from him.

Christine Winters: That's great. As you know, there are two sections in our department, the Asian Section and the European Section. We have a significant market share in Europe. And the Asian section has been newly established for the purpose of exploring new international market. Actively exploring Asian market has become important strategic decision of our company. Would you like to join in the Asian market team?

Daniel Zheng: I'd like to.

Christine Winters: With the development of China, Chinese market has been the core challenge for us. Are you ready to explore Chinese market with sharp sense of touch? Are you ready to develop market with our high quality product, and occupy market with our honest service?

Daniel Zheng: Of course. I can hardly wait to plunge into my work now.

Christine Winters: I'd like to you to meet everybody first. Come on.

(Christine Winters and Daniel Zheng come into the Asian Section Office of the International Sales Department.)

Christine Winters: Good morning, everyone. There's someone I'd like you to meet. This is Daniel Zheng, he is our new international salesperson. He comes from China, and he is excellent in sales. Daniel, this is Andrew Hard. He is the director of Asian Section.

Andrew Hard: Hello, Daniel, it's nice to meet you. Welcome to our group.

Daniel Zheng: I'm glad to meet you too.

Christine Winters: This is Amelia Hill. She deals with Japanese and Korean market.

Amelia Hill: Hi, pleased to see you Daniel.

Daniel Zheng: Nice to see you, Amelia.

Amelia Hill: If there's anything I can do for you, let me know.

Daniel Zheng: Thanks.

(Ella finger comes in with a pile of files.)

Ella Finger: Excuse me, Mrs. Winters. You have an appointment with Mr. White. He is waiting for you in the conference room on the second floor.

Christine Winters: Oh, yeah. I have to go now. Daniel, you have met Ella Finger, our secretary?

Daniel Zheng: Yeah. Nice to see you again, Ella.

Ella Finger: Nice to see you again, Daniel.

Christine Winters: Ella, would you like to show Daniel around instead of me?

Ella Finger: Of course.

Christine Winters: Daniel, if you have any questions, don't hesitate to ask Ella. You'll find all the resources you need to make your job a smooth one. It's time to go now. Have a good day, Daniel.

Daniel Zheng: Have a good day. Mrs. Winters.

Task 2 Being Familiar with the Work Environment

Ella Finger: Daniel, let me show you around.

Daniel Zheng: Thank you very much.

Ella Finger: Here is your cubicle. And here are some files for you, including company brochure, product catalogue, job description, employee handbook, client information and so on. You can read them first before you begin to work.

Daniel Zheng: Thanks a lot.

Ella Finger: This is your telephone. The number is 213-345-9125. The yellow book is over there. Here is your computer. The password is IS9837-3656, which is also your employee number. Please keep it in mind. And you'd better change the password as soon as possible.

Daniel Zheng: Yes, I will.

Ella Finger: You can apply for office stationary at the back office.

Daniel Zheng: Where is the back office?

Ella Finger: I'll show you, it is just opposite to our office. Come this way. Our back office is just over there. And you can also borrow equipment for presentations there, for example, the over-head projector, notebook computers, tape recorder, micro-phone and so on. Come this way. The European section office is just on the other side of manager's room. The conference rooms are all on the first floor and the second floor. Mrs. Winters is talking with Mr. White on the second floor. Do you know Mr. White?

Daniel Zheng: No, I don't know.

Ella Finger: He is the manager of Product Department. Now the Product Department and Logistic Department are both on the first floor. The Customer Service Department and the R&D Department are on the second floor. The Domestic Sales Department and our department are on the third floor. The CEO's office, the HR Department, Administrative and Financial Department are on the top floor.

Daniel Zheng: Oh, I see.

Ella Finger: Here is the rest room. There's a water cooler, and a coffeemaker. The sofa is over there.

Daniel Zheng: That's great.

Ella Finger: And this is a copy machine, and that is a fax machine. We can have a drink and have a break while we make copies.

Daniel Zheng: Humanity Design! Oh, Excuse me, could you show me how to use the copy machine?

Ella Finger: Let me show you how to operate the copy machine. First of all, make sure that there is paper. The next thing you have to do is to put the document down, face down like this. And then indicate how many copies you want. Finally press the button. OK, so is that clear?

Daniel Zheng: Sure, but could you tell me how to make two-sided copies.

Ella Finger: These directions will show you how to make two-sided copies and how to make bulk copies.

Daniel Zheng: Oh, that's great.

Ella Finger: Let's get back to the office.

Daniel Zheng: OK.

Ella Finger: Don't forget to clock in and clock out. Our office hours are from 9:00 a.m. to 5:00 p.m. with one hour for lunch at 11:30 a.m. Do you have any other questions?

Daniel Zheng: Yeah, what day is payday?

Ella Finger: We get paid on the 7th of very month. Oh, by the way, the back office is going to print Name Card and Badge for you, you can call them. The number of back office is 213-345-9118.

Daniel Zheng: Thank you, Ella.

Ella Finger: You're welcome. Call me anytime you have a problem. See you later.

Daniel Zheng: See you.

Task 3 Designing Business Card and ID Badge

Rainbow Pet Products Corp., Los Angeles, California

Daniel Zheng

International Salesperson, International Sales Department

Address: 1358 Westwood Blvd, Los Angeles, CA90024-4911, USA
Tel: 213-345-9125
Fax: 213-345-9125
E-mail: danielzheng@yahoo.com

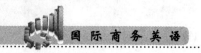

Daniel Zheng

International Salesperson, International Sales Department

Daniel Zheng

IS9837-3656

 Knowledges

International Macro-environments

The company and all of the other actors operate in a larger macro-environment of forces that shape opportunities and pose threats to the company. There are six major forces in the international macro-environments.

Natural environments are the natural resources needed as inputs by marketers or that are affected by marketing activities.

Economic environments are the factors that affect consumer buying power and patterns.

Demographic environments are the monitors population in terms of age, sex, race, occupation, location and other statistics.

Technological environments are the forces that create new product and market opportunities.

Political environments are the laws, agencies and groups that influence or limit marketing actions.

Cultural environments are the forces that affect a society's basic values, perceptions, preferences, and behaviors.

Practice: Match Column I with Column II.

I	II
1. Shortages of Raw Material	A. Demographic environments
2. Changes in Income	
3. Increased Legislation	B. Economic environments
4. Rapid Pace of Change	
5. Higher Pollution Levels	C. Natural environments
6. Views That Express Values	
7. Increased Management	D. Technological environments
8. Increased Costs of Energy	
9. Changes in Consumer Spending Patterns	E. Political environments
10. Growing Ethnic and Racial Diversity	
11. Changing Age Structure	F. Cultural environments

International Micro-environments

International Micro-environment are the actors close to the company that affect its ability to serve its customers, which includes 5 factors.

Suppliers provide the resources needed to produce goods and services.

Marketing Intermediaries help the company to promote, sell, and distribute its goods to final buyers.

Customers are markets that purchase a company's goods and services.

Competitors are those who serve a target market with similar products and services.

Publics are any group that perceives itself having an interest in a company's ability to achieve its objectives. It includes financial publics, media publics, government publics, citizen-action publics, local publics, gereral public, and internal publics.

Practice: Match Column I with Column II.

I	II
1. newspaper	A. Financial publics
2. managers	

3. stockholders	B. Media publics
4. consumer organizations	
5. neighborhood residents	C. Government publics
6. public image	
7. banks	D. Citizen-action publics
8. board of directors	
9. radio and television stations	E. Local publics
10. community organizations	
11. magazine	F. General publics
12. workers	
13. investment houses	G. Internal Publics
14. environment groups	
15. taxes	

Skills Requirements

Vocabulary: Office Facilities

 Fill in the forms with the words below.

wastepaper basket/bin; notice board; video cassette recorder (VCR); board marker; scissors; stapler; shredder; typewriter; swivel chair; (book) shelf; (desk) lamp; telephone; pencil holder; answering machine; carousel socket; remote control; desk/chair; photocopier; calculator; overhead projector; laser/inkjet printer; franking machine; staple; in tray/in box; lectern VDU (visual display unit); file/folder; flip chart; out tray/out box; paper clip; slide projector, digital video camera; printer paper; stationery cupboard; (electric) pencil sharpener; (ball point) pen/biro; microphone; filing cabinet; rubber/eraser; elastic band/rubber band; notepad; notebook; message pad; desk diary; cassette (tape) recorder (player); headed paper; appointment diary; computer (PC)/desktop; phone/telephone book; directory/yellow pages; typing paper; window envelope

Module Three Working Environment

Office Furniture	
Office Equipment/ Facilities	
Office Stationary	

Listening: Asking for Directions

 Listen to the dialogues twice, and choose the best answers.

1. Where is the largest department Store?
A. At the left side of the crossroads.
B. At the right side of the crossroads.
C. At the East of the crossroads

2. Where is the Bank?
A. In the middle of the post office and the shopping mall.
B. On the right of the Cherry Avenue.
C. Adjacent to the shopping mall.

3. Which sentence is right?
A. It takes 15 minutes to go to the hospital by car.
B. The hospital is just at the second traffic lights.
C. The second traffic lights is three blocks away from the hospital.

4. How can Jack go to the Simpson Hall?
A. By taxi.
B. On foot.
C. By train.

5. Which sentence is right?
A. The Holiday Inn is near the bus stop of No.403 bus.
B. They are going to the Holiday Inn together on foot.

C. The big sign of the Holiday Inn can be seen at the bus stop of No.407 bus.

Speaking: First Day at Work

Work in pairs with a partner. Look at the question. Take one minute to prepare your answer. Think of reasons to explain your choice. Then tell your partner your answer and reasons.

WHAT IS IMPORTANT FOR …?
Your first day at work

- Smile a lot and be friendly
- Arrive early
- Dress neatly

Reading: Starting a New Job

 Fill in the blanks after reading the article.

Starting a New Job[1]

Your first day is here. That time off sure flew by, didn't it? Put on the one suit that you know makes you shine. If you feel confident, you'll look confident to others. Whether you're driving to work or using mass transit, be sure to leave plenty of time to get there early. Treat it like a job interview, and remember first impressions do count. Eat breakfast before you leave your house — fresh breath and clean teeth are a must.

Your work day begins when you leave your house. You never know when you'll come into contact with your co-workers or boss. A friend of mine was driving to work one day when a car swung around her and the driver made a hand gesture at my friend. He didn't see my friend's face, but she saw his. It looked familiar and then my friend remembered why. He was her most recent hire, starting work that very day. She attributed his action to nerves, and hasn't said a word to him. Yet, you shouldn't make lewd hand gestures regardless of who the recipient may be, but if you are tempted to, just think of the other person as being a potential boss, co-worker, or client.

So you finally made it to your new workplace. Now take a deep breath and walk in with a smile on your face. Keep your head up and remember to make eye contact. Be polite and friendly to everyone you encounter, whether it's the receptionist or the mailroom clerk, your colleagues or your new boss. Introduce yourself to those you meet and remember that it's okay to ask questions. People generally like to help others and it usually makes them feel good about themselves. I remember a new co-worker who refused all offers of help. I guess she thought it would make her look incompetent to our boss. The result was that everyone thought she was a snob or a know-it-all and some people even vowed to refuse to help her in the future.

---

1. By Dawn Rosenberg McKay, About.com Guide.

Module Three **Working Environment**

While it's okay to hold onto some of things you learned in your previous jobs and use that knowledge in your new job, remember that every workplace has it's own way of doing things. Your first few weeks or even months on a job is not the time to change the way things get done. Do not utter these words: "That's not how we did it at my old company." Your colleagues will just be thinking this: "Well, you're not at your old company and if you liked it so much why didn't you stay there."

The length of time it takes you to adjust to a new job varies from person to person, and job to job. While you may fit in immediately at some jobs, it may take a little longer in others. And some people seem to fit in immediately wherever they go. All you can do is try your best, and do your job the best way you know how. The following tips may help:

Ask questions. You're new and it's better to do something right the first time around than have to do it over.

Smile a lot and be friendly. Get to know your co-workers and what their interests are.

Use your lunch hours to get together with your current co-workers, although it may be tempting to meet up with your former ones.

Figure out who has the authority to give you work to do and who is just trying to have you do theirs. I worked with a woman who would try to push off her work on any unsuspecting person. It took a while to realize that she didn't have the authority to hand out assignments.

Pay attention to the grapevine, but don't contribute to it. You don't want to gain a reputation as a gossip monger.

Don't complain about your boss, your office mate, any co-workers, or your previous job.

Continue to arrive early and don't rush out of the door at the end of the day.

Volunteer for projects that will help you get noticed, but don't neglect any assigned work.

Keep a positive attitude and an open mind. Your life has changed and it will take getting used to.

Do	Don't

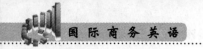

Writing: Note

You have an important appointment with a client for three hours. You have to go now. But you are waiting for an important phone call from Mr. Johnson, the provider of office equipment. Leave a note for your secretary Sharon.

- Say where you are
- Say when you will be back
- Tell her to ask him to send the catalogue and instructions of the office equipment if Mr. Johnson calls

(30-50 words)

Module Four
Company and Product

导入案例
　　你适合创业吗?

任务要求
　　学生分成五人一组,分别扮演新员工、老员工、公司部门经理及秘书,用英文介绍公司、产品和企业结构。

任务流程
　　1. 新员工写公司简介。
　　2. 新员工向老员工了解产品。
　　3. 新员工向老员工了解公司组织结构。

知识要点
　　1. 公司的类型。
　　2. 跨国企业。
　　3. 福布斯世界五百强企业。
　　4. 产品。

技能要求
　　1. 词汇:公司名称、产品和服务。
　　2. 听:沃尔玛。
　　3. 说:创建新公司。
　　4. 读:宜家。
　　5. 写:麦当劳。

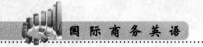

Leading In

Should You Be an Entrepreneur? [1]

Just answer yes or no. Be honest with yourself — remember from my last post: the worst lies are the ones we tell ourselves.

I don't like being told what to do by people who are less capable than I am.
I like challenging myself.
I like to win.
I like being my own boss.
I always look for new and better ways to do things.
I like to question conventional wisdom.
I like to get people together in order to get things done.
People get excited by my ideas.
I am rarely satisfied or complacent.
I can't sit still.
I can usually work my way out of a difficult situation.
I would rather fail at my own thing than succeed at someone else's.
Whenever there is a problem, I am ready to jump right in.
I think old dogs can learn — even invent — new tricks.
Members of my family run their own businesses.
I have friends who run their own businesses.
I worked after school and during vacations when I was growing up.
I get an adrenaline rush from selling things.
I am exhilarated by achieving results.
I could have written a better test than Isenberg (and here is what I would change ....)

Task Requirements

The students are divided into groups with 5 members each. Student A plays a role as the new staff. Student B plays a role as the secretary of the International Sales Department. Student C plays a role as the manager of the International Sales Department. Student D and E play the roles as the coworkers in the department. They will finish the tasks together as follows.

---

1. Based on http://blogs.hbr.org/cs/2010/02/should_you_be_an_entrepreneur.html By Daniel Isenberg.

Module Four   *Company and Product*

Task 1 Writing the Company Profile

Company Profile is the concise description which includes company's name, type, product/service offered, history, location, number and quality of its employees, reputation, anticipated performance and the contact method.

Student A plays a role as Daniel Zheng, the new international salesperson in the International Sales Department of Rainbow Pet Products Co., Ltd., Los Angeles, California. He is writing the company profile according to the following Questions.

 Write the company profile according to the following Questions.

- What is the name of the company?(Rainbow Pet Products Co., Ltd., Los Angeles, California)
- What is the type of the company? (Private Limited Liability Company)
- Where is the Company located? (Los Angeles)
- How many employees does the company have? (more than 500 employees)
- What is the product offered? (professional Pet Nutrition and Pet Supplies)
- What is the most famous product? (Rainbow Milk Replacers)
- When is it established? (1993)
- What do you know about the reputation of the company? (one of the leaders in the pet product industry.)
- What will it continue to do? (to provide quality products and services with honesty, integrity, and gratitude)
- How to get in touch with them? (1358 Westwood Blvd, Los Angeles, CA90024-4911, USA Tel: 213-345-9125 Fax: 213-345-9125 E-mail:danielzheng@yahoo.com)

Company Profile

Contact:

63

Task 2 Introducing the Product

Catalog is the list of items available for purchase, with the product item number, title of the product, brief product description.

Catalogs are intended for use by salesperson and contain a complete listing of all products sold by that company. Some catalogs use elaborate photographic techniques and settings in order to present their goods attractively.

Product Description is a structured format of presenting information about a product printed on the packing or in the product description brochure. The structure includes title, purpose, net weight, product facts, direction, cautions and warnings.

Student A plays a role as Daniel Zheng, the new international salesperson in the International Sales Department of Rainbow Pet Products Co., Ltd., Los Angeles, California.

Student D plays a role as Andrew Hard, the director of the Asian section of International Sales Department of Rainbow Pet Products Co., Ltd., Los Angeles, California.

Andrew Hard gives a brief introduction of the product Categories to Daniel Zheng according to Table 4-1 and Table 4-2. Daniel asks a few questions about the star products, and the difference between the products for cats and dogs.

Table 4-1 Catalog

Catalog Rainbow Pet Products Co., Ltd., Los Angeles, California					
Dogs Products Rainbow has multiple solutions for your dog's health needs.					
Catogaries	Item No.	Title	Description	Remarks
Multivitamins	DV-101	Pet Chews™ PLUS D3 for Dogs	Maximum Daily Vitamin & Mineral Support for Dogs 60 Liver Flavored chewables	
	DV-102	Puppy Chews™	Complete Daily Multi-Vitamin & Mineral Supplement for Puppies 90 Liver Flavored Chewables	
Milk Replacer	DM-101	Milk Replacer for Dogs	Enriched with Colostrum Food Supplement for Puppies & Pregnant or Lactating Dogs Net Wt. 12 Oz.	
	DM-102	Milk Replacer for Dogs (Lg)	Enriched with Colostrum Food Supplement for Puppies & Pregnant or Lactating Dogs Net Wt. 28 Oz.	

Module Four *Company and Product*

Catogaries	Item No.	Title	Description	Remarks
Cat Products Rainbow has multiple solutions for your cat's health needs.				
Multivitamins	CV-101	Pet Chews Calcium D3	Daily Calcium Supplement for Cats 180 Flavored Chewables	
	CV-102	Kitten Chews™	Complete Daily Multi-Vitamin & Mineral Supplement for Puppies 90 Liver Flavored Chewables	
Milk Replacer	CM-101	Milk Replacer for Cats Enriched with Colostrum	Food Supplement for Kittens & Pregnant or Lactating Cats Net Wt. 12 Oz.	
	CM-102	Milk Replacer for Cats	Enriched with Colostrum Food Supplement for Kittens & Pregnant or Lactating Cats Net Wt. 6 Oz.	

Table 4-2 Product Description for Rainbow Milk Replacer

Rainbow Milk Replacer Page 25

Formulated specifically to nourish and enrich orphaned animals and lactating mothers. Milk Replacers provide the nutrients necessary for a thriving, healthy young puppy/kitten.

Milk Replacer for Dogs (DM-101)
Enriched with Colostrum
Food Supplement for Puppies & Pregnant or Lactating Dogs
Net Wt. 12 Oz.
Product Facts
For Newborn Puppies to 6 Weeks of Age
Guaranteed Analysis:
CRUDE PROTEIN, min .33%
CRUDE FAT, min 40.0%
CRUDE FIBER, max 5.0%
MOISTURE, max 10.0%
   The calorie content is 900 kcal/kg or 13.5 kcal/Tbs when reconstituted 1:2 12 oz. can of powder makes approximately 60 oz. of formula when mixed 1:2.
   Ingredients: Vegetable Oil, Whey Protein Concentrate, Sodium Caseinate, Dried Skim Milk, Butter Fat, Egg Yolk, Monocalcium Phosphate, L-Arginine, dl-Methionine, Potassium Chloride, Choline Chloride, Lecithin,

Calcium Carbonate, Silicon Dioxide, Zinc Sulfate, Magnesium Carbonate, Ferrous Sulfate, Sodium Chloride, Vitamin E Supplement, Magnesium Sulfate, Dried Colostrum, Ascorbic Acid, Niacin, d-Calcium Pantothenate, Copper Sulfate, Manganese Sulfate, Vitamin A Supplement, Riboflavin, Pyridoxine Hydrochloride, Thiamine Hydrochloride, Vitamin D3 Supplement, Folic Acid, Vitamin B12 Supplement, Potassium Iodide, Biotin

Directions

All puppies should receive their mother's milk for at least 2 days, if possible. This first milk gives extra nutrition and temporary immunity against some diseases. Warm reconstituted formula to room or body temperature (Do not use a microwave to warm reconstituted formula). Feed puppies 2 tablespoons of liquid (30 mL) per 4 oz. (115 g) of body weight.

The daily feeding rate should be divided into equal portions for each feeding. The puppy's needs will vary and this amount may have to be increased or decreased, depending on the individual. Small or weak puppies may need to be fed every 3 to 4 hours, while larger and/or older puppies do well when fed formula every 8 hours. Weigh the puppies daily to assure adequate feeding.

Cautions

Reconstituted formula must be kept refrigerated for up to 24 hours. Opened powder must be refrigerated for up to 3 months or can be frozen for up to 6 months.

Warnings

Consult your veterinarian for additional advice. Not for human consumption. When a food supplement is desired for growing postweaned puppies, show dogs, supplementing large litters, and old, or convalescent dogs, powder should be fed at the rate of 1 teaspoon per 5 lbs. (2.2 kg) body weight. If Puppy develops diarrhea, does not gain weight, cries constantly, or becomes lethargic, take to a veterinarian.

Mixing Directions: Gently shake or stir 1 part into 2 parts warm water. Do not mix more than can be consumed in 24 hours. Mix until all lumps are dissolved. Do not use a blender. Do not feed if formula is warmer than room or body temperature.

PREGNANT AND LACTATING DOGS: Mix powder into the daily ration at the rate of 2 teaspoons per 5 lbs. (2.2 kg) of body weight until 2 weeks after whelping.

Milk Replacer for Cats (CM-101)

Enriched with Colostrum

Food Supplement for Kittens & Pregnant or Lactating Cats

Net Wt. 12 Oz.

Product Facts

For Newborn Kittens to 6 Weeks of Age

Guaranteed Analysis:

CRUDE PROTEIN, min .42%

CRUDE FAT, min 25.0%

CRUDE FIBER, max 5.0%

MOISTURE, max 10.0%

The calorie content (ME) is 740 kcal/kg or 11.1 kcal/Tbs when reconstituted 1:2.

12 oz. can of powder makes approximately 60 oz. of formula when mixed 1:2.

Module Four Company and Product

> Ingredients: They Protein Concentrate, Vegetable Oil, Dried Skim Milk, Butter Fat, Sodium Caseinate, Egg Yolk, Corn Syrup Solids, Monocalcium Phosphate, L-Arginine, Potassium Chloride, Choline Chloride, Calcium Carbonate, Lecithin, Magnesium Carbonate, Ferrous Sulfate, L-Taurine, Magnesium Sulfate, Vitamin E Supplement, Dried Colostrum, Zinc Sulfate, Manganese Sulfate, Copper Sulfate, Niacin, Vitamin A Supplement, Ascorbic Acid, d-Calcium Pantothenate, Thiamine Hydrochloride, Pyridoxine Hydrochloride, Riboflavin, Folic Acid, Potassium Iodide, Vitamin B12 Supplement, Biotin, Vitamin D3 Supplement
>
> **Directions**
> All kittens should receive the mother's milk for at least 2 days, if possible. This first milk gives extra nutrition and temporary immunity against some diseases. Warm reconstituted formula to room or body temperature (Do not use a microwave to warm reconstituted formula). Feed kittens 2 tablespoons (30 mL) of liquid per 4 ounces (115 g) of body weight. The daily feeding rate should be divided into equal portions for each feeding. The
>
> **Cautions**
> Reconstituted formula must be kept refrigerated for up to 24 hours. Opened powder must be refrigerated for up to 3 months or can be frozen for up to 6 months.
>
> **Warnings**
> Consult your veterinarian for additional advice. Not for human consumption. When a food supplement is desired for growing postweaned kittens, show cats, and old or convalescent cats, powder should be fed at a rate of 1 teaspoon per 5 lbs. (2.2 kg) of body weight. If kitten develops diarrhea, does not gain weight, cries constantly, or becomes lethargic, take to a veterinarian.
>
> Mixing Directions: Gently shake or stir 1 part into 2 parts warm water. Do not mix more than can be consumed in 24 hours. Mix until all lumps are dissolved. Do not use a blender. Do not feed if formula is warmer than room or body temperature.
>
> PREGNANT AND LACTATING cats: Mix powder into the daily ration at the rate of 2 teaspoons per 5 lbs. (2.2 kg) of body weight until 2 weeks after queening.

 Simulate the situation according to the above information.

Task 3 Introducing the organizational structure

Organizational Structure is the framework, within which an organization arranges its lines of authority and communications, and allocates rights and duties. Organizational structure determines the manner and extent to which roles, power, and responsibilities are delegated, controlled, and coordinated, and how information flows between levels of management.

Student A plays a role as Daniel Zheng, the new international salesperson in the International Sales Department of Rainbow Pet Products Co., Ltd., Los Angeles, California.

Student E plays a role as Amelia Hill, the international salesperson in the Asian Section of the International Sales Department of Rainbow Pet Products Co., Ltd., Los Angeles, California.

Daniel Zheng asks for Amelia's helps to learn the organizational structure of the company. Amelia Hill introduced the organizational structures to Daniel Zheng according to Table 4-3.

Table 4-3 Name List

Position	Name
CEO	Doris Green
CFO	Sophia Green
Chief human resources officer	Bridges Thompson
International Sales Department Manager	Christine Winters
Domestic Sales Department Manager	George Fox
R&D Department Manager	Harper Short
Customer Service Manager	Isabel Longman
Product Department Manager	Paul White
Logistics Department Manager	Lee Wood
Back Office Manager	Mary Carter

 Simulate the situation according to the above information.

 Task Process

Task 1 Writing the Company Profile

Company Profile

Rainbow Pet Products Co., Ltd., Los Angeles, California is a Private Limited Liability Company specialized in Pet Products. It is a high-tech, modern enterprise dealing with professional pet nutrition and pet supplies. It is originally founded in 1993 in Los Angeles, USA, with more than 500 employees. It is to be recognized as one of the leaders in the Pet Products industry.

The Rainbow Milk Replacers have become the most favorite products in American and European market which delivering health and wellness to cats and dogs. Many cats and dogs had grown up with the Rainbow brand.

Rainbow Pet Products Co., Ltd., Los Angeles, California continues to provide a wide array of quality products and services with honesty, integrity, and gratitude.

Contact:
Address: 1358 Westwood Blvd, Los Angeles, CA90024-4911, USA
Tel: 213-345-9125
Fax: 213-345-9125
E-mail: danielzheng@yahoo.com

Module Four Company and Product

Task 2 Introducing the Product

Andrew Hard: Daniel, here is the Catalog and Product Description. Please read it. As you know it is necessary for us to be familiar with the products we sell.

Daniel Zheng: I'd like to. But would you please tell me which one is the star product of our company?

Andrew Hard: Of course. There are two major categories of products in our company. One is professional Pet Nutrition such as Multivitamins and Milk Replacer. The other is Pet Supplies such as pet beds, pet clothes and pet staff toys. But we are famous for the Pet Nutrition, because the Rainbow science and research team takes the lead in creating nutrition solutions for cats and dogs.

Daniel Zheng: Then there are two kinds of nutrition products, Multivitamins and Milk Replacer.

Andrew Hard: That's right. The Multivitamins are mature products in the product life cycle. But the Milk Replacer is the star product of our company backed by high quality, market longevity, and good support. Milk Replacers provide the nutrients necessary for a thriving, healthy young puppy or kitten. It becomes the world famous nutritionally balanced formula for feeding puppies. We'll try our best to push the Rainbow Milk Replacer to the Asian market.

Daniel Zheng: So we should pay more attention to the Milk Replacer. Then is there any differences in the Milk Replacer for dogs and cats?

Andrew Hard: Of course, there is. The crude protein is 33% and crude fat is 40% for dogs. But the crude protein is 42% and crude fat is 25% for dogs. The products are developed differently to adapt to the different levels of physical ability of dogs and cats.

Daniel Zheng: And for the same purpose, the Ingredients are different too.

Andrew Hard: That's right. If you have any questions, don't hesitate to tell me.

Daniel Zheng: Thanks a lot.

Task 3 Introducing the organizational structure

Daniel Zheng: Excuse me, Amelia, would you like to give me a hand?

Amelia Hill: Of course, I'd glad to.

Daniel Zheng: Would you please introduce the organizational structure of our company.

Amelia Hill: Sure. As you know, our CEO is Doris Green. He is the founder of our company. He built the company from nothing when he was 24 years old. He is a legend here and has lots of admirers all over the company.

Daniel Zheng: Are you one of the admirers.

Amelia Hill: Of course. There are 8 departments in our company. They are Administrative

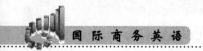

and Financial Department, HR Department, Domestic Sales Department, R&D Department, Customer Service Product Department, Logistics Department and our department.

Daniel Zheng: What is the meaning of CFO?

Amelia Hill: CFO is the Chief Financial Officer, who is in charge of Administrative and Financial Department.

Daniel Zheng: What is the Administrative and Financial Department comprised?

Amelia Hill: The Administrative and Financial Department includes various sections, such as Accounting, Tax, and Payroll.

Daniel Zheng: Who is the CFO?

Amelia Hill: Sophia Green, she is the CEO's wife. As she loves pets, Mr. Green established the company for her. What a romantic story!

Daniel Zheng: So, our company is a family corporation.

Amelia Hill: You may well say so.

Daniel Zheng: What Is the HR Department?

Amelia Hill: HR Department makes up the workforce of the company. It is responsible for the attraction, selection, training, assessment, and rewarding of employees, while also overseeing organizational leadership and culture, and ensuring compliance with employment and labor laws. You must have met Bridges Thompson, who recruited you into our company. He is a nice man.

Daniel Zheng: He is really friendly.

Amelia Hill: You have been familiar with our department. Christine Winters is full of energy and enthusiasm. She seems never to lose her youthful vigor. We all love her.

Daniel Zheng: Me too.

Amelia Hill: Domestic Sales Department is on the same floor with us. George Fox is responsible for the Domestic Sales Department. There are two sections there, the East and the West. The Sales figure of the West section is three times more than that of us last year. But this year, it's different. We got a big order last month.

Daniel Zheng: Congratulations.

Amelia Hill: Thanks. And if you have a good relationship with R&D Department, Product Department, Customer Service Department and Logistic Department, you'll do the job at twice the speed and with half the effort.

Daniel Zheng: Thank you for your advice.

Amelia Hill: Have you applied for the office stationary?

Daniel Zheng: Not yet.

Amelia Hill: Mary Carter in the back office is my best friend. Would you like to come with me? I'd like to introduce you to her.

Daniel Zheng: That's wonderful. Thank you very much.

Amelia Hill: You are welcome. Come on.

Module Four *Company and Product*

Types of Company

Company is a voluntary association formed and organized to carry on a business. It is an association or collection of individual real persons and/or other companies, who each provide some form of capital. Two types of companies may be incorporated under the act, namely non-profit companies and profit companies.

Non-profit Companies (NPC) is a company incorporated for public benefit or other object relating to one or more cultural or social activities, or communal or group interests; and the income and property of which are not distributable to its incorporators, members, directors, officers or persons related to any of them. A nonprofit organization uses its profit to improve its services, rather than pay dividends to investors.

Profit Companies may be divided into the following types:

Sole Proprietorship (SP) is the particular business owned by a single individual and all the related business decisions are taken by the person.

Partnership is a type of business ownership where two or more people shares the ownership of the company and the profits or losses are equally divided among these owners. All of them are motivated by the common goal.

Limited Liability Company (LLC) is a business ownership that combines the limited personal liability feature of a corporation with the single taxation feature of a partnership or sole-proprietorship firm. Also called company limited by share or limited company.

Incorporation (Inc.) is also called Corporation which is an entity that is separate from its owners, so that regardless of what happens to shareholders, the corporation continues until it is legally dissolved.

Public Limited Companies (PLC) is a type of business ownership that has very little amount of liability. These companies have a lot of shareholders.

Practice: Make a comparison of Five Business Structure Alternatives.

	Owner	Limited Liability	Legal and administration costs	Private or Public	Field
SP					
Partner					
LLC					
Inc.					
PLC					

Multinational Corporation

Multinational Corporation (MNC) is an enterprise operating in several countries but managed from one (home) country. Generally, any company or group that derives a quarter of its revenue from operations outside of its home country is considered a multinational corporation.

There are four categories of multinational corporations: a multinational, decentralized corporation with strong home country presence; a global, centralized corporation that acquires cost advantage through centralized production wherever cheaper resources are available; an international company that builds on the parent corporation's technology or R&D; a transnational enterprise that combines the previous three approaches.

Practice: Match Column I with Column II.

I	II
1. A Parent company	A. is an enterprise controlled by another (called the parent) through the ownership of greater than 50 percent of its voting stock.
2. A Subsidiary	B. is an office of a firm which is located somewhere other than the firm's main office location.
3. A State-owned Enterprise (SOE)	C. is a firm that owns or controls other firms (called subsidiaries) which are legal entities in their own right.
4. Branch Office	D. is a firm incorporated under the laws of a foreign jurisdiction and owned or controlled by non-nationals.
5. Foreign Corporation	E. is a business operating under a privilege granted to make or market a good or service under a patented process or trademarked name.
6. Franchise	F. is a business that is either wholly or partially owned and operated by a government.

Fortune Global 500

The Fortune Global 500, also known as Global 500, is an annual ranking of the top 500 corporations worldwide as measured by revenue.

The list is compiled and published annually by Fortune magazine with data on the firm's assets, net earnings, earnings per share, number of employees, etc.

Fortune is a global business magazine published by Time Inc.'s Fortune & Money Group. It was founded by Henry Luce in 1930. The magazine is actually famous for this list. The first Fortune 500 list was published in 1955. Until 1989 it listed only non-US industrial corporations under the title "International 500", while the Fortune 500 contained and still contains exclusively US corporations. In 1990, US companies were added to compile a truly global list of top industrial corporations as ranked by sales. Since 1995, the list has had its current form, listing also top financial corporations and service providers by revenue. The Fortune Global 500 list is one of the most important buzzwords for trade and commerce. The Top 10 companies in 2012 is according to Table 4-4.

Table 4-4 Top 10 Companies published in 2012

Rank	Company	Country	Industry	2011 revenue in USD
1	Royal Dutch Shell	Netherlands	Petroleum	$484.4 billion
2	Exxon Mobil	United States	Petroleum	$452.9 billion
3	Wal-Mart Stores	United States	Retail	$446.9 billion
4	BP	United Kingdom	Petroleum	$386.4 billion
5	Sinopec	China	Petroleum	$375.2 billion
6	China National Petroleum	China	Petroleum	$352.3 billion
7	State Grid	China	Power	$259.1 billion
8	Chevron	United States	Petroleum	$245.6 billion
9	ConocoPhillips	United States	Petroleum	$237.2 billion
10	Toyota Motor	Japan	Automobiles	$235.3 billion

Practice: Have a group discussion on the Global 2011 and 2010 compared with 2012 above. And answer the following questions according to Table 4-5.

Question 1: What have been changed in the list?

Question 2: What happened to Wal-Mart Stores?

Question 3: How did the Chinese Company Performed?

Table 4-5 Top 10 Companies published in 2011 and 2010[1]

	2011	2010
1	Wal-Mart Stores	Wal-Mart Stores
2	Royal Dutch Shell	Royal Dutch Shell
3	Exxon Mobil	Exxon Mobil
4	BP	BP
5	Sinopec Group	Toyota Motor
6	China National Petroleum	Japan Post Holdings
7	State Grid	Sinopec
8	Toyota Motor	State Grid
9	Japan Post Holdings	AXA
10	Chevron	China National Petroleum

---

1. It is published on 9 July 2012. It is based on the companies' fiscal year ended on or before 31 March 2012, which have been released by the magazine at its website.

Product

A product is a good or service that most closely meets the requirements of a particular market or segment and yield enough profit to justify its continued existence.

Product Life Cycle is the four distinct but not wholly-predictable stages every product goes through from its introduction to withdrawal from the market: introduction, growth in sales revenue, maturity, during which sales revenue stabilizes, and decline, when sales revenue starts to fall and eventually vanishes or becomes too little to be viable. The Product Life Cycle is according to Chart 4-1.

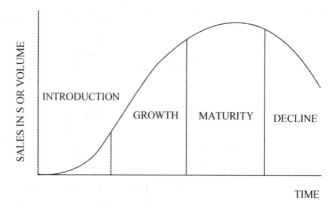

Chart 4-1 Product Life Cycle

Three Levels of a Product was suggested by P. Kotler[1] that a product should be viewed in three levels, which are the core product, the actual product, and finally the augmented product as follows (Chart 4-2).

The core product is the dominant benefit or satisfaction that a customer expects from a good or service he or she buys.

The Actual Product is the tangible aspects of a product, such as the brand name, design, features, quality level, styling.

The Augmented Product is also called agile product. The additional products and services may be added to generate multiple revenue streams to the core product.

---

1. Philip Kotler (born 27 May 1931 in Chicago) is an American academic focused on marketing. The author of Marketing Management among dozens of other textbooks and books. The nine volume Legends in Marketing: Philip Kotler published in 2012 collects over 150 of his articles, with critical commentary.

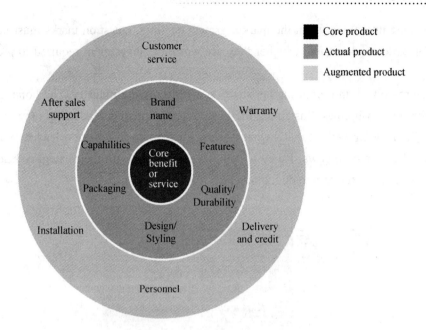

Chart 4-2 Three Levels of Products[1]

The Boston Matrix is a chart that had been created by Bruce Henderson for the Boston Consulting Group in 1970 to help corporations with analyzing their business units or product lines. This helps the company allocate resources and is used as an analytical tool in brand marketing, product management, strategic management, and portfolio analysis.

Cash cows are units with high market share in a slow-growing industry. These units typically generate cash in excess of the amount of cash needed to maintain the business. They are regarded as staid and boring, in a "mature" market, and every corporation would be thrilled to own as many as possible. They are to be "milked" continuously with as little investment as possible, since such investment would be wasted in an industry with low growth.

Dogs, or more charitably called pets, are units with low market share in a mature, slow-growing industry. These units typically "break even", generating barely enough cash to maintain the business's market share. Though owning a break-even unit provides the social benefit of providing jobs and possible synergies that assist other business units, from an accounting point of view such a unit is worthless, not generating cash for the company. They depress a profitable company's return on assets ratio, used by many investors to judge how well a company is being managed. Dogs, it is thought, should be sold off.

Question marks (also known as problem children) are growing rapidly and thus consume large amounts of cash, but because they have low market shares they do not generate much cash. The result is a large net cash consumption. A question mark has the potential to gain market share and become a star, and eventually a cash cow when the market growth slows. If the question mark does not succeed in becoming the market leader, then after perhaps years of cash consumption it

---

1. Dibb et al. (2001, p.254)

will degenerate into a dog when the market growth declines. Question marks must be analyzed carefully in order to determine whether they are worth the investment required to grow market share.

Stars are units with a high market share in a fast-growing industry. The hope is that stars become the next cash cows. Sustaining the business unit's market leadership may require extra cash, but this is worthwhile if that's what it takes for the unit to remain a leader. When growth slows, stars become cash cows if they have been able to maintain their category leadership, or they move from brief stardom to dogdom, which described in Chart 4-3.

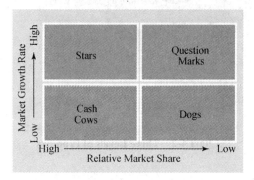

Chart 4-3　Boston Matrix

Practice: Fill in the form with letter A to U.

Introduction (A seed is planted.)	
Growth (It begins to sprout.)	
Maturity (It shoots out leaves and puts down roots as it becomes an adult)	
Decline (The plant begins to shrink and die out.)	

A: In this stage, it may be appropriate to tweak the products by adding new features. In this way the competition may be fended off. It may also make sense to reduce prices a little to bring in more price sensitive consumers.

B: As a product moves to this stage, the product is old and dated. Its pricing, promotion, packaging, and distribution are re-evaluated and changed.

C: At this point competition is strong and margins may begin to suffer.

D: The marketplace may be unfamiliar with the product and creating awareness takes time.

E: The stage is characterized by a rapid increase in sales volume.

F: Advertising spend is high and focuses upon building brand.

Module Four *Company and Product*

G: Those products tend to spend longest in this phase.

H: At this point there is a downturn in the market.

I: Competitors are attracted into the market with very similar offerings.

J: Consumer tastes have changed.

K: Products become more profitable and companies form alliances, joint ventures and take each other over. Market share tends to stable.

L: There is intense price-cutting and many more products are withdrawn from the market.

M: Sales grow at a decreasing rate and then stable.

N: Profits can be improved by reducing marketing spend and cost cutting.

O: Producers attempt to differentiate products and brands are key to this. Price wars and intense competition occur.

P: Producers begin to leave the market due to poor margins.

Q: The need for immediate profit is not a pressure.

R: The product is promoted to create awareness.

S: If the product has no or few competitors, a skimming price strategy is employed.

T: Promotion becomes more widespread and use a greater variety of media.

U: At this point the market reaches saturation.

Fill in the form with letter A to G.

Level 1 Core Product	
Level 2 Actual Product	
Level 3 Augmented Product	

A: John Lewis a retail departmental store offers free five year guarantee on purchases of their Television sets.

B: I bought the camera in order to purchase memories.

C: Mary loves LV bags. She believes LV is an icon in itself and has made the brand a status symbol.

D: You can go where you like, when you want to, and travel around relatively quickly after you buy a car.

E: We aim to maintain high standards of customer service.

F: Changing the packaging is a tired brand's last refuge.

G: Another core benefit is speed.

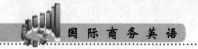

Skills Requirements

Vocabulary: Company

Fill in the full name of the top 10 Companies of Global 500 with the words below.

> Company; Plc; Group; Corp; Inc.

1. Royal Dutch Shell _____
2. Exxon Mobil _____
3. BP _____
4. Wal-Mart Store, _____
5. China National Petroleum _____
6. Sinopec _____
7. State Power Grid _____
8. Chevron _____
9. ConocoPhillips _____
10. Toyota Motor _____

Fill in the full name of the following Companies with the words below.

> House; Lines; Associates; System; Office; Service; Center; Airlines; Agency

1. Columbia Broadcasting _____
2. British Nuclear _____
3. Independent Design _____
4. China Southern _____
5. Atlantic Container _____
6. China Youth Travel _____
7. China Ocean Shipping _____
8. Windsor House Shopping _____
9. 3M China Limited Guangzhou Branch _____

Module Four   Company and Product

Vocabulary: Products and Services

Match Column I with Column II.

I	II
1. Insurance	A. Products are anything that can be offered to a market for attention, acquisition, use or consumption and that might satisfy a need or want.
2. Car	
3. Renting	
4. Mobile phone	
5. Book	
6. Home stay	B. Services are activities or benefits offered for sale that are essentially intangible and don't result in the ownership of anything.
7. Haircut	
8. Massage	
9. Taxi	
10. Milk	

Listening: Wal-Mart Stores Inc.

Listen to the passage twice, Choose the best answer according to what you have listened.

1. How many employees are there in Wal-Mart worldwide?
   A. More than 2.0 million   B. More than 2.1 million   C. Less than 1.4 million
2. When was Wal-Mart founded by Sam Walton?
   A. 1962   B. 1969   C. 1972
3. When did Wal-Mart trade on the New York Stock Exchange?
   A. 1962   B. 1969   C. 1972
4. Which of the following was not mentioned?
   A. Wal-Mart Stores Inc. is the world's biggest retailer.
   B. The company is the world's largest public corporation, according to the Fortune Global 500 list in 2011.
   C. Wal-Mart remains a family-owned business.
5. Which of the following was true?
   A. Wal-Mart has 8,500 stores in 16 countries, under 55 different names.
   B. Wal-Mart reported sales of $443.9 billion for fiscal 2012.
   C. Net income for the entire company was $15.8 billion in fiscal 2012.

6. Which one got the biggest revenues?

A. Wal-Mart stores

B. Sam's Club

C. International stores

7. Which one increased most from the previous year?

A. Wal-Mart stores

B. Sam's Club

C. International stores

8. Which one is highly successful?

A. Ventures in Germany

B. Ventures in South Korea

C. Ventures in China

Speaking: Establishing a Company

Work in pairs with a partner. Look at the question. Take one minute to prepare your answer. Think of reasons to explain your choice. Then tell your partner your answer and reasons.

WHAT IS IMPORTANT WHEN …?
Establishing a company

- Name
- Ownership
- Business Scope

Reading: IKEA

Read the passages below. What are the main ideas of the passages below. Choose from A-D.

IKEA

1.

IKEA is a world wide furnishing company with operations in 42 countries and a total number of 70 000 employees of which 59 000 work in Europe. It is a Swedish based company built on the idea to "offer a wide range of well-designed, functional home furnishing products at prices so low, that as many people as possible will be able to afford them".

2.

IKEA started out in the 1940s by the entrepreneur Ingvar Kamprad, who still has control over the company through the INGKA foundation, situated in the Netherlands. The IKEA group is solely owned by the Foundation through a holding company (INGKA holding B.V). It is therefore not listed on any stock exchange.

3.

> It is important to realize the business IKEA is in and its strategy to be successful in that business. The dominating business process is distribution and retailing. The closeness to the customer is of utmost importance. The strategy is built on joint design and cost-effective distributions processes. There is also a hard pressure on suppliers to be cost-effective in their operations.

4.

> IKEA has had a great expansion, establishing a number of new stores every year during the last decade, and also moving into new countries, even though Europe still is the main market. The transnational issues in a company like IKEA is not the relocation of jobs, moving operations to the most cost-effective country or region. The stores have to be where the customers are. Opening and closing of stores are strategic decisions and often initiated from the holding company in the Netherlands, but the carrying out are local initiatives.

A: The global expansion

B: The general introduction

C: The business strategy

D: The ownership

Writing: Company Profile of McDonald's Plaza

 Write a Summary according to the passage below.

> **McDonald's Plaza**[1]
> Oak Brook, Illinois 60523-2199
> U.S.A.
>
> Company Perspectives:
> McDonald's is the world's leading food service organization. We generate more than $40 billion in Systemwide sales. We operate over 30,000 restaurants in more than 100 countries on six continents. We have the benefits that come with scale and a strong financial position. We own one of the world's most recognized and respected brands. We have an unparalleled global infrastructure and competencies in restaurant operations, real estate, retailing, marketing and franchising. We are a leader in the area of social responsibility. We actively share our knowledge and expertise in food safety and are committed to protecting the environment for future generations. Yet, we have not achieved our growth expectations for the past several years. So, our challenge is to leverage our strengths to profitably serve more customers more ways more often.
> Since its incorporation in 1955, McDonald's Corporation by Ray Kroc has not only become the world's largest quick-service restaurant organization, but has literally changed Americans' eating habits—and increasingly the habits of non-Americans as well. On an average day, more than 46 million people eat at one of the company's more than 31,000 restaurants, which are located in 119 countries on six continents. About 9,000 of the restaurants are company owned and operated; the remainder are run either by franchisees or through joint ventures with local businesspeople. Systemwide sales (which encompass total revenues from

---

1. Based on http://www.fundinguniverse.com/company-histories/mcdonald-s-corporation-history/.

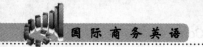

all three types of restaurants) totaled more than $46 billion in 2003. Nine major markets—Australia, Brazil, Canada, China, France, Germany, Japan, the United Kingdom, and the United States—account for 80 percent of the restaurants and 75 percent of overall sales. The vast majority of the company's restaurants are of the flagship McDonald's hamburger joint variety. Two other wholly owned chains, Boston Market (rotisserie chicken) and Chipotle Mexican Grill (Mexican fast casual), along with Pret A Manger (upscale prepared sandwiches), in which McDonald's owns a 33 percent stake, account for about 1,000 of the units.

 Write a Summary with the following information.
- What's the name of the company
- Type of Company
- What's the Business Scope?
- When was the company established?
- Who was the founder?
- What was the notable success?

(no more than 50 words)

Module Five
Regular Meeting

导入案例

你是哪一种团队成员？

任务要求

学生分成五人一组，分别扮演新员工、老员工、公司部门经理及秘书，用英文完成一次部门例会。

任务流程

1. 部门秘书按照部门经理要求安排会议时间和会议室。
2. 部门秘书撰写会议议程。
3. 部门秘书发送会议通知。
4. 部门经理组织召开例会。
5. 部门秘书撰写会议记录。

知识要点

1. 团队合作。
2. 国际市场营销和国际销售。
3. 市场营销计划和营销组合。
4. 图表。

技能要求

1. 词汇：需要、想要和需求、产品和服务、营销术语、图表用语。
2. 听：赛百味营销组合。
3. 说：柱形图。
4. 读：加拿大就业情况。
5. 写：折线图。

Leading In

Which team member are you? [1]

How do I contribute to the team? Which one do you choose.

A: I come up with great ideas for the project.

B: I help to work out exactly what to do and who does what.

C: I like to organize the things and information we need for the project

D: I'm good at listening to others and working hard to finish the task in order to make sure others are happy.

E: I know how to do things that others in the team don't.

F: I make sure everyone stays on track and the project gets done properly and on time and I check that there are no mistakes.

Task Requirements

The students are divided into groups with 5 members each. Student A plays a role as the new staff. Student B plays a role as the secretary of the International Sales Department. Student C plays a role as the International Sales Department manager. Student D and E play the roles as the coworkers in the department. Student F plays a role as the back office manager. They will finish the tasks together as follows.

Task 1 Arranging a Regular Meeting

Meeting arrangements include who will participant in the meeting, where and when it will be hold and what is the topic of the meeting. The time and venue reserved in advance should be in accordance with the requirements of meeting. The purpose of the meeting will influence the choice of the venue. A formal meeting should be held in a formal venue as this will encourage formal behavior. An informal meeting should be held in a relaxed atmosphere. Usually, a regular meeting will take place at the same time and location on each occasion.

Student B plays a role as Ella Finger, the secretary of the International Sales Department of Rainbow Pet Products Co., Ltd., Los Angeles, California.

Student C plays a role as Christine Winters, the manager of the International Sales Department of Rainbow Pet Products Co., Ltd., Los Angeles, California.

---

1. based on http://www.belbin.com/downloads/Belbin_Team_Role_Summary_Descriptions.pdf.

Module Five *Regular Meeting*

Student F plays a role as Mary Carter, the back office manager of Rainbow Pet Products Co., Ltd., Los Angeles, California.

Christina Winters asks Ella Finger to arrange a regular meeting of this month talking about the performance of Asian Section last month and the work in progress at 9:00 a.m. on Nov. 6th, 2012 at meeting room 204 with a projector. And she asks Ella Finger to inform all the staff in Asian Section and prepare an agenda for the regular meeting.

Ella Finger calls Mary Carter, the back office manager to reserve the meeting room. But Mary Carter tells her that the meeting room has been reserved, and asks her whether she could change a date or a venue. After discussion with Christina Winters, they decide to hold the meeting at meeting room 106 with a round table.

 Simulate the situation according to the above information.

Task 2 Writing an Agenda

Agenda is a list of items to be discussed in a formal meeting. An agenda indicates what prior knowledge would be expected from the participants, and indicates what outcome the participants may expect from the meeting.

Student B plays a role as Ella Finger, the secretary of the International Sales Department of Rainbow Pet Products Co., Ltd., Los Angeles, California. She writes an agenda for a meeting according to the requirements in Task 1.

 Fill in the blanks with the following information.
- Participants
- The name of the writer
- Date of the agenda
- Type of the meeting
- Venue
- Time of the meeting
- Participants
- Objectives
- Contents

```
To:
From:
Date:
              AGENDA OF THE REGULAR MEETING
          TO BE HELD AT   ON              , IN ROOM
Agenda:
```

85

> Confirmation of the meeting notes of the last meeting.
> Participants:
> Principal Objectives:
> Contents:
> The First Item:
> The Second Item:
> The Third Item:
> Conclusion

Task 3 Writing a Meeting Notice

Meeting notice is a notification sent to staff of a company, informing them of a time, date, and location of a meeting.

Participants will be able to contribute more effectively if they are well prepared. They need to know: the subject and purpose of the meeting, the agenda for the meeting, have sufficient pre-meeting access to important documents, what is expected of them, time and place of the meeting, and how long it is expected to last.

Student B plays a role as Ella Finger, the secretary of the International Sales Department of Rainbow Pet Products Co., Ltd., Los Angeles, California.

She posts a meeting notice for a meeting on an office bulletin board according to the requirements in Task 1.

 Fill in the blanks with the following information.

- Date of posting the notice
- Participants
- Venue
- Time
- Date
- Department

> **Meeting Notice**
>
> _____
>
> All the _____ is required to attend the meeting at _____ on _____, at _____, _____.
>
> Please prepare to make a speech of the performance last month with sales figures and everyone's work in progress.
>
> _____

Module Five *Regular Meeting*

Task 4 Holding a Regular Meeting

Regular Meetings are held at definite times, at a definite place, and usually for a definite duration to follow an agreed upon agenda. A regular meeting involves management and employees, such as planning meeting, and sales meeting. A meeting is typically headed by a chairperson, and its deliberations are recorded in a written form called minute.

Meetings generally follow a more or less similar structure and can be divided into five parts, which are introducing, reviewing, beginning, discussing, and finishing. The holder should hold the meeting as follows.

- Welcoming and introducing participants
- Stating the principal objectives of a meeting
- Giving apologies for someone who is absent
- Reading the minute of the last meeting
- Dealing with recent developments
- Introducing the agenda
- Allocating roles
- Agreeing on the ground rules for the meeting (contributions, timing, decision-making, etc.)
- Introducing the first item on the agenda
- Closing an item
- Giving control to the next participant

…

- Summarizing
- Suggesting and agreeing on time, date and place for the next meeting
- Thanking participants for attending
- Closing the meeting

Student A plays a role as Daniel Zheng, the new international salesperson of International Sales Department of Rainbow Pet Products Co., Ltd., Los Angeles, California.

Student B plays a role as Ella Finger, the secretary of the International Sales Department of Rainbow Pet Products Co., Ltd., Los Angeles, California.

Student C plays a role as Christine Winters, the manager of International Sales Mepartment of Rainbow Pet Products Co., Ltd., Los Angeles, California.

Student D plays a role as Andrew Hard, the director of the Asian section of International Sales Department of Rainbow Pet Products Co., Ltd., Los Angeles, California.

Student E plays a role as Amelia Hill, the international salesperson in the Asian Section of the International Sales Department of Rainbow Pet Products Co., Ltd., Los Angeles, California.

Ella Finger hands out the agenda to the participants and she takes notes and finishes the minute after the meeting. Christine Winters holds the meeting according to the agenda. Andrew Hard introduces the performance of Asian Section according to the following Chart 5-1 And he decides to pay more attention to Chinese market. And Amelia Hill continues to be responsible for maintaining the established market. And Daniel Zheng takes his first steps into his job by making a market research.

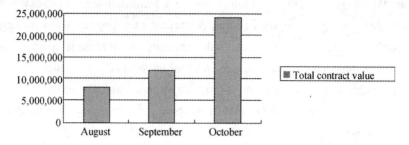

Chart 5-1　The Total Contract Value of August, September and October

Simulate the situation according to the above information.

Task 5　Writing a Minute

Minute is a detailed record of meetings. It typically describes the events of the meeting, starting with a list of attendees, a statement of the issues considered by the participants, and related responses or decisions for the issues. Minute may be created during the meeting by a secretary, who may take notes, with minute prepared later.

Student B plays a role as Ella Finger, the secretary of the International Sales Department of Rainbow Pet Products Co., Ltd., Los Angeles, California. She takes notes and creates the minute for the meeting according to Task 4 (5.2.4).

Fill in the minute with the following information.
- Time
- Venue
- Last meeting contents
- Participants
- Secretary
- Participants
- Absent
- Contents
- Conclusion (summarizing and decision making)
- Date and time of the next meeting

Module Five *Regular Meeting*

MINUTE

Date:
Meeting place:
Last meeting contents:
Principal objectives:
Secretary:
Participants:
Absent persons' name:
Agenda:
The First Item:

The Second Item:

The Third Item:

Summarizing

Decision making:

Date and Place for the Next Meeting

 Task Process

Task 1 Arranging a Regular Meeting

Christine Winters: Ella, would you like to reserve the meeting room 204 for the regular meeting of Asian Section talking about the performance of Asian Section last month and the work in progress.

Ella Finger: What time will it be held?

Christine Winters: At 9:00 a.m. on Nov. 6th, 2012.

Ella Finger: Sure. How long will it last?

Christine Winters: Just under 1 hour. And everyone in Asian Section needs to say something about their work in progress. Please tell Andrew to bring their latest sales figures. Pass this notice along, please. And prepare an agenda for the meeting.

Ella Finger: That's ok. I'll reserve the meeting room first and convey the information to the Asian Section.

Christine Winters: That's great. And don't forget to arrange the drinks for the participants.

Ella Finger: Tea or coffee?

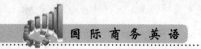

Christine Winters: It's up to you.

Mary Carter: Back Office. This is Mary Carter. What can I do for you?

Ella Finger: Mary, this is Ella Finger from International Sales Department. I want to book a meeting room for a one-hour regular meeting?

Mary Carter: Which one do you like?

Ella Finger: We usually hold the regular meeting at meeting room 204?

Mary Carter: When do you like to use?

Ella Finger: At 9:00 a.m. on Nov. 6th, 2012.

Mary Carter: Let me see. Oh, it is a pity that it has been reserved by the R&D department from 9:00 to 11:00. Would you like to change the time or change the room?

Mary Carter: Hold on please. Mrs. Winters, the room 204 has been reserved. Would you like to change the time or the room?

Christine Winters: I'm afraid the time couldn't be changed. Are there any other meeting rooms available?

Ella Finger: Mary, do you have another room with a projector?

Mary Carter: Let me check. Yeah, there is a meeting room with a projector which can hold ten people. It's room 106 with only one round table and ten chairs. Is that OK?

Ella Finger: Mrs. Winters, there is a meeting room with a projector, one round table and ten chairs. Is that OK?

Christine Winters: OK.

Ella Finger: Mary, I'd like to reserve the meeting room 106 from 9:00 a.m. to 10:00 a.m. on Nov. 6th, 2012.

Mary Carter: Meeting room 106 from 9:00 a.m. to 10:00 a.m. on Nov. 6th, 2012. Is that right?

Ella Finger: Yeah.

Mary Carter: Is there any other machine do you need?

Ella Finger: No, thanks. A projector is enough. We'll take our own laptop. Thanks a lot.

Mary Carter: My pleasure. See you.

Ella Finger: See you. Mrs. Winters, it's done.

Christine Winters: Good Job. Please print 5 copies of the agenda after you finish it.

Ella Finger: I'll finish it before 4 o'clock this afternoon and I'll send you one copy in advance.

Christine Winters: Thanks.

Task 2 Writing an Agenda

To: All of the Asian Section of International Sales Department
From: Ella Finger, the secretary of the International Sales Department
Date: Nov. 1st, 2012

AGENDA OF THE REGULAR MEETING
TO BE HELD AT 9:00 a.m. ON Nov. 6th, 2012, IN ROOM 106

Agenda:
Confirmation of the meeting notes of the last meeting.
Participants: Christine Winters, Andrew Hard, Amelia Hill, Daniel Zheng, Ella Finger.
Principal Objectives: Performance of Asian Section and work in progress
Contents:
The First Item: Performance of Asian Section last month by Andrew Hard.
The Second Item: Work in progress by Amelia Hill.
The Third Item: Work in progress by Daniel Zheng.
Conclusion

Task 3 Writing a Meeting Notice

Meeting Notice
Nov. 1st, 2012

All the staff in Asian Section of International Sales Department is required to attend the meeting in the Meeting Room 106 on Tuesday, at 9:00 am, Nov.6th, 2012.

Please prepare to make a speech of the performance last month with sales figures and everyone's work in progress.

International Sales Department

Task 4 Holding a Regular Meeting

(Everyone is ready for the meeting.)

Christine Winters: Good morning, everyone. If we are all here, let's get started. I'd like to extend a warm welcome to all of you, Andrew, Amelia, Daniel and Ella. We're here today to talk about our performance last month and our work in progress. Ella, would you like to hand out the agenda?

(Ella hands out the agenda.)

Christine Winters: Has everyone received the agenda? If there is nothing else we need to discuss, I'd like to quickly go through the minute of our last meeting, which was held on Oct., 6th, 2012. We have talked about the new marketing plan. And it works. I have heard of your brilliant performance. Are there any questions about the marketing plan? If not, let's advance the marketing plan with renewed efforts.

OK, it's time for today's agenda. We are talking about our performance last month with detailed sales figure and our work in progress. If you don't mind, I'd like to go in order today. Ella, would you mind taking the minute?

Ella Finger: I'd like to.

Christine Winters: Andrew, would you like to kick off? Can you tell us how about the performance of the Asian Section last month?

Andrew Hard: Good morning, everyone. I'd like to give you a brief introduction of the performance of our Asian Section last month. Here's the bar chart of the detailed sales figure. The bar chart shows the total contract value we have obtained last month compared with August, September. The x axis indicates months. The y axis indicates the total contract value. The bar represents August, September, and October respectively. Last month, we have obtained five orders from South Korea and three orders from Japan, and one from china. We can see from the bar chart that the total contract value mounts to USD 24,000,000, which is twice as much as Sept. and three times as much as August. In general, the new marketing plan has increased foreign sales. And it recently made its first big deal in China.

Christine Winters: That's great. But a good performance one month tends not to be repeated the next. You will need to work harder to get the attention of our core clients.

Andrew Hard: Yes, we will.

Christine Winters: And then how's your work going?

Andrew Hard: As you know we have obtained a Big order from china unexpected. I recognize the astonishing potential market in China. I am taking my time to sound out the potential market, to understand what Chinese customers need in terms of types of Pet Products and to figure out how to organize our sales force.

Christine Winters: So do I. Let's cheer for our team. Amelia, how about you?

Amelia Hills: Andrew has told me that he is going to pay more attention to the new market in China. And he asks me to maintain the customer relationship with the old clients. A good customer relationship is unique. My responsibility is to build, recover, and strengthen the customer relationships in the market of Japan and South Korea.

Christine Winters: That's right. We're in an industry in which we constantly have to make new markets. But loyal customers are as valuable as the gold. Maintaining our established market is as important as exploring new market. How is Daniel going along with your new work?

Daniel Zheng: Andrew was really having me do some market research first. I'd like to be familiar with the business and cultural issues, understand the market of China of first hand data,

Module Five Regular Meeting

through market research.

Christine Winters: That's great. If you have done this, you have taken the first step for success. Research should always be your first step.

Before we close today's meeting, why don't we quickly summarize what we've done today. Andrew decides to pay more attention to Chinese market. And Amelia is responsible for maintaining the established market. And Daniel takes his first steps into his job. We have done a great job. What has happened is incredible, but we should keep on working very hard in the future and we can expect more miracles to happen.

Is there Any Other Business? If there are no other comments, I'd like to wrap this meeting up. Can we set the date for the next meeting, please? So, the next meeting will be on Monday, Dec. 3rd, 2012. Thank you all for attending. The meeting is finished. See you later.

All: See you.

Task 5 Writing a Minute

MINUTE

Date: 9:00 a.m. on Nov. 6th, 2012
Meeting place: In room 106
Last meeting contents: Marketing plan
Principal objectives: Performance of Asian Section last month and the work in progress
secretary: Ella Finger
Participants: Christine Winters, Andrew Hard, Amelia Hill, Daniel Zheng, Ella Finger.
Absent persons' name: None
Agenda:
The First Item: Performance of Asian Section last month by Andrew Hard.
"Last month, we have obtained five orders from South Korea and three orders from Japan, and one from china. We can see from the bar chart that the total amounts of the contracts mounts to USD 240,000, which is twice as much as Sept and three times as much as August."
"I am taking my time to sound out the potential market, to understand what Chinese customers need in terms of types of Pet Products and to figure out how to organize our sales force."
The Second Item: Work in progress by Amelia Hill.
"My responsibility is to build, recover, and strengthen the customer relationships in the market of Japan and South Korea."
The Third Item: Work in progress by Daniel Zheng.
"I'd like to be familiar with the business and cultural issues, understand the market of China of first hand data, through market research."
Summarizing: "Andrew decides to pay more attention to Chinese market. And Amelia is responsible for maintaining the established market. And Daniel takes his first steps into his job."
Decision making: "What has happened is incredible, but we should keep on working very hard in the future and we can expect more miracles to happen."
Date and Place for the Next Meeting: on Monday, Dec. 3rd, 2012.

Knowledges

Team Building

Team building is a philosophy of job design in which employees are viewed as members of interdependent teams instead of as individual workers. Team building is an important factor in any environment, its focus is to specialize in bringing out the best in a team to ensure self development, positive communication, leadership skills and the ability to work closely together as a team to solve problem.

Practice: Think about how you usually act in teams. Complete these tables. Compare your answers with those from others in your team.

Team Work Skills[1]	Rank these skills from 1 to 7 1 = my strongest skill 7 = my weakest skill
Listening: I listen to my team's ideas and use their ideas to help get new ones	
Questioning: I ask questions of my team to help work out what to do and to learn more.	
Persuading: I express my ideas and try to explain my thinking to my team.	
Respecting: I respect the opinions in my team. I offer encouragement and support for new ideas and efforts.	
Helping: I help my team by offering my assistance.	
Sharing: I share with my team. I make sure I share my ideas and thinking. I share the jobs.	
Participating: I contribute to the team assignment. I am actively involved with the work.	

International Marketing and International Sales

International Marketing is the performance of business activities that direct the flow of a company's goods and services to consumers or users in more than one nation for a profit.

It is the process by which individuals and groups obtain what they need and want through creating and exchanging products and value with others carried out by companies overseas or across national borderlines. Marketing activities include consumer research (to identify the needs of the customers), product development (designing innovative products to meet existing

---

1. based on http://www.griffith.edu.au/centre/gihe/griffith_graduate/toolkit/.

Module Five *Regular Meeting*

or latent needs), advertising the products to raise awareness and build the brand. The typical goal of marketing is to generate interest in the product and create leads or prospects. Marketing is more proactive where you promote your audience. Marketing focuses on helping clients meet their business goals and objectives. Marketing is everything that you do to reach and persuade prospects.

International Sales are the transaction in which the buyer and the seller are from different nations. Sales activities are focused on converting prospects to actual paying customers. Sales involve directly interacting with the prospects to persuade them to purchase the product. Sales are more reactive. Sales focus more on the product. The sales process is everything that you do to close the sale and get a signed agreement or contract.

Practice: Fill in the blank with A-L.

	International Marketing	International Sales
Starting Point:		
Focus:		
Means:		
Process:		
Horizon:		
Ends:		

A: Existing Product
B: One to many
C: Selling and Promoting
D: Factory
E: Short term
F: Profits through Volume
G: Customer Needs
H: Integrated Marketing
I: Usually one to one
J: Longer term
K: Market
L: Profits through Satisfaction

Marketing Plan

A **marketing plan** outlines the specific actions you intend to carry out to interest potential customers and clients in your product and/or service and persuade them to buy the product and/or services you offer. It included summary, current market situation, threatening and opportunities, objectives and issues, marketing strategy, action program, finance and control.

Summary is the agenda of the marketing plan which is the complete converge of each section of your plan. The summary assists the reader in understanding your plan.

Current market situation gives introduction of product background and product history.

Threatening and opportunities can be organized into market analysis including market size, market growth, market potential and forecast, market segments, consumer behavior, competitor analysis including competitor descriptions, competitor strategies, and company SWOT analysis.

Objectives include sales revenues, market share, profits, return on investment, customer satisfaction, customer repeat purchases, salesperson quotas, growth in distribution outlets, sales by specific distribution outlet.

Marketing Strategy is a broad directional statement that describes how marketing objectives will be accomplished which includes market positioning, target segment and marketing mix.

Action program defines as specifically as possible the detailed actions, timing and implementation of the marketing mix including product, promotion, price, and place (distribution) as appropriate to the situation in order to reinforce brand, strengthen customer loyalty and extend product, develop new segment and extend distribution points.

Finance is the budget for the marketing action.

Controls are useful when assumptions underlying the market plan have a significant degree of uncertainty or risk which include alternative action plans.

The marketing mix is a business tool used in marketing products. The marketing mix is often crucial when determining a product or brand's unique selling point (the unique quality that differentiates a product from its competitors), and is often synonymous with the four Ps: price, product, promotion, and place, which is showed in chart 5-2.

Chart 5-2　Marketing Mix

Product is the products or services offered to your customer. Some examples of product decisions include brand name, functionality, styling, quality, safety, packaging, repairs and support, warranty, accessories and services.

Price is how your price remains competitive but allows you to make a good profit. Some examples of price decisions include retail price, volume discounts and wholesale pricing, cash and early payment discounts, seasonal pricing, bundling, price flexibility and price discrimination.

Module Five Regular Meeting

The cost of transport, tariffs or import duties, exchange rate fluctuations, personal disposal incomes of the target market, the currency they want to be paid in and the general economic situation of the country and how this will influence pricing.

Place (Also referred to as Distribution) is where your business sells its products or services and how it gets those products or services to your customers. Some examples of distribution decisions include: distribution channels, market coverage, specific channel members, inventory management, warehousing, distribution centers, order processing, transportation, and reverse logistics.

Promotion is the method used to communicate the features and benefits of your products or services to your target customers which consists of five major tools, advertising, direct marketing, sales promotion, public relationship, and personal selling.

Practice: Fill A-P into Column II.

I	II
Product	
Price	
Promotion	
Place	

A: McDonald's restaurants seem to be located on every high street throughout the UK.

B: Frequent special offers are made, such as the very successful "two for the price of one Big Mac" offer in 1999.

C: The extensive use of standardization throughout its operations.

D: In 1974 the original advertising slogan promised "There's a difference at McDonald's you'll enjoy".

E: Advertising on television and in national newspapers is designed to reflect the humorous side of the British way of life, with McDonald's at its centre.

F: Staff training, food and drink products, packaging and the design and decoration of restaurants are consistent in all of their outlets.

G: In 1996 the company reached a ten-year agreement with Disney for the exclusive rights to merchandise based on new Disney films such as A bug's Life and Pocahontas.

H: Offering catering as a leisure experience.

I: Point-of-sale displays and posters are also used at outlet so entice hungry passers-by.

J: McDonald's has continuously developed new products to meet changing customer needs.

H: Offering catering as a leisure experience.

K: In 1998 the company spent £44 million on advertising campaigns compared to the £15.6 million spent by their competitor Burger King.

L: Trends in healthy eating and the growing popularity of vegetarianism have led to the introduction of fish and bean burgers.

M: The development of Indian-style products.

N: The company has also developed outlets at airports, on ferries, at football grounds and even in hospitals.

O: The development of the hugely successful Happy Meals offering food, a soft drink and a free toy.

P: Undertakes a great deal of sponsorship, particularly sporting events such as NASCAR racing and the France '98 World Cup.

Charts

Depending on the information that analysts are seeking there are many types of charts.

Line Charts are used to track changes over short and long periods of time.

Pie Charts can be used to compare parts of a whole. The percentages of a whole can be shown and represented at a set point in time. Line charts can also sued to compare changes over the same period of time for more than one group.

Bar Charts are used to compare things between different groups or to track changes over time. They can be used for different items in a related category.

Candlestick Charts are similar to a bar chart as it provides the same four bits of data in each entry. The hollow or filled portion of the candlestick is called "the body". The long thin lines above and below the body represent the high/low range and are called "shadows" (also referred to as "wicks" and "tails").

Practice: Choose the best answer from A, B and C.

1. Chart 5-3 is an example of _____.

A. Line chart

B. Bar chart

C. Pie chart

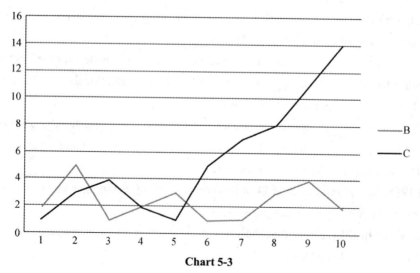

Chart 5-3

2. Chart 5-4 is an example of _____.

A. Line chart

B. Bar chart

C. Candlestick chart

Chart 5-4

3. Chart 5-5 is an example of _____.

A. Line chart

B. Bar chart

C. Candlestick chart

Chart 5-5

4. Chart 5-6 is an example of _____.

A. Line chart

B. Bar chart

C. Pie chart

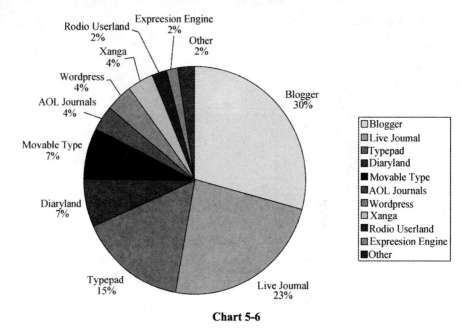

Chart 5-6

Skills Requirements

Vocabulary: Needs, Wants and Demands

 Match Column I with Column II

I	II
1. I want a bottle of mineral water.	A. Needs are the state of felt deprivation for basic items such as food and clothing and complex needs such as for belonging.
2. I am tired. But I have to go back home.	
3. I have money to buy a bottle of mineral water.	B. Wants from that a human need takes as shaped by culture and individual personality.
4. I need to go by bus.	
5. I am thirsty.	C. Demands are human wants backed by buying power.
6. I have $10 in my pocket to go by bus.	

Module Five *Regular Meeting*

Vocabulary: Marketing Terms

 Match Column I with Column II.

Terms	Definition
1. Customer Value	A. Some who is interested in buying, but may not.
2. Customer Satisfaction	B. The benefit that the customer gains from owning and using a product compared to the cost of obtaining the product.
3. potential buyer	C. The product's perceived performance in delivering value relative to a buyer's expectations.
4. actual buyer	D. Someone who is committed to buying a product

Vocabulary: Charts Description

 Fill in the forms with the following words.

> flourish, get up, go up, grow, advance, catch up, add to, decrease, compress, curtail, peak at, lessen, reduce, shorten, drop, dive, lapse, progress, raise, mount, enlarge, expand, extend, have a wavy line or appearance, smooth, plunge, tumble, give up, come around, get back, get better, heal, improve, reclaim, regain, at the top of, at the bottom of, descend, decline, destroy, collapse, ruin, remain steady, retrieve, rescue, even, flat, constant, horizontal, level off, wavelike motion, ascend, rise, have a wavelike appearance/face/form, gain, increase, vary irregularly, rise and fall, increase and decrease, undulate, wave, move in waves or with a smooth, all, defeat, overthrow, cut, diminish, recover, revive, recuperate.

101

Listening: Marketing Mix of Subway

 Choose the best answer according to what you have listened.

1. Subway is a Multinational Transportation Franchise?
   A. True   B. False   C. Not mentioned
2. Sandwiches and Salads are the main products of Subway?
   A. True   B. False   C. Not mentioned
3. The Price of subway is quite high?
   A. True   B. False   C. Not mentioned
4. Subway are all in the commercial area.
   A. True   B. False   C. Not mentioned
5. Subway has the same promotional activities as McDonalds and KFC.
   A. True   B. False   C. Not mentioned

Speaking: Bar Chart

 Describe the Chart 5-7 using the sentences below.

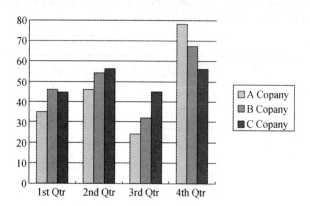

Chart 5-7　The Sales of Three Companies

- Opening

  Good afternoon, everyone.

  Welcome to the presentation of…

  I want to begin by…

  I would like to mention briefly

- Topic

  This …graph/chart shows/illustrates/demonstrates…

  Here is a …graph/chart showing…

  What we have here is a …graph/chart showing…

This bar chart shows the growth…

Here is a graph showing the growth …

This diagram focuses on the growth…

- Representation

    Each bar on the chart represents the growth in our sales.

    These three pie wedges each present…

    The wedges on this pie graph illustrate the growth in our sales.

    The x axis represents…

    The y axis indicates…

- Comparison

    The bar of … is as long/short as the bar of…

    The bar of … is longer/shorter than the bar of…

    The wedge of …is as big/small as the wedge of…

    The wedge of …is bigger/smaller than the wedge of…

    The point of … is as high/low as the point of…

    The point of … is higher/lower than the point of…

    The longest bar is…

    This group of thin wedges shows…

    The lowest point on the graph is…

- Opinion

    It seems to me that…

    In my opinion, …

    From my experience, …

    As far as I can see…

    I prefer to…

    First of all, …

    Secondly, …

    Turning to…

    Furthermore, …

    IN addition, …

    On the one hand …, but on the other hand…

    In spite of…, I still think …

    Finally, …

- Conclusion

    If this pattern (trend) continues…, …

    If this trend holds…, …

    One of the conclusions is…

    One of the implications is…

    In summary then…

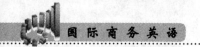

On the whole…
In general…
By and large, …
Generally speaking, …
Keys: free

Reading: Employment of Canada

 Draw a bar chart according to the following description and data[1]

Employment of Canada

This is a bar chart.
There are in total 7 categories in the horizontal axis. The vertical axis starts at 16,400 and ends at 17,600 with ticks every 200 points.
There are 1 series in this graph.
The vertical axis is "thousands".
The units of the horizontal axis are months by year ranging from January 2009 to May 2012.
The title of series 1 is "Employment".
The minimum value is 16,743.8 occurring in July 2009.
The maximum value is 17,357 occurring in January 2012.
Employment

Month	Thousands
January 2009	16,909.7
July 2009	16,743.8
January 2010	16,882.9
July 2010	17,088
January 2011	17,227.9
July 2011	17,340.1
January 2012	17,357

Writing: Description of a Line Chart

Describe the bar chart according to Chart 5-8 which shows Harry's sales of Hamburgers in 1998 (100-150 words).

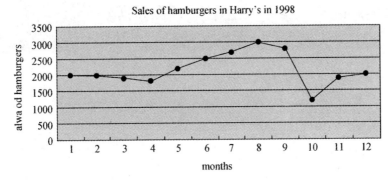

Chart 5-8　Sales of Hamburgers in Harry

Module Six
Customer Reception

导入案例

　　商务礼仪误区测试。

任务要求

　　学生分成六人一组，分别扮演新员工及其主管、部门经理、公司总裁、客户以及某酒店前台用英文完成一次客户邀请和接待任务。

任务流程

　　1. 部门经理向客户发出邀请函，邀请客户参加公司二十周年庆典，并附上日程表，请柬。
　　2. 客户发确认函确认出席。
　　3. 新员工到机场接机并将客户送入酒店。
　　4. 在欢迎晚宴上，互相介绍问候，公司总裁致词。

知识要点

　　1. 文化。
　　2. 商务礼仪。

技能要求

　　1. 词汇：手势。
　　2. 听：就餐礼仪。
　　3. 说：接受邀请的注意事项。
　　4. 读：iPone5的发布促使苹果股价上扬。
　　5. 写：请柬。

Module Six *Customer Reception*

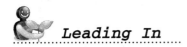 Leading In

Business Etiquette Blunders Quiz [1]

Have you ever wished you knew more about business etiquette at holiday dinners, interview luncheons, and award banquets? Knowing some essential tips can help you benefit from these opportunities without worrying about eating from the wrong salad bowl or not properly introducing your guest to your boss. Test your knowledge of business etiquette with the short quiz below.

Questions:

1. A business meal is a time to relax and "let loose." True or false
2. Whose name do you say first when introducing your spouse to your boss? Spouse or Boss
3. Clothing is never neutral. It either adds or detracts from a professional image. True or false
4. A man should wait for a woman in business to extend her hand for a handshake. True or false
5. A drink should be held in the right hand at a cocktail party. True or false
6. Where would you find your salad plate? To the right of the entrée plate or to the left of the entrée plate
7. Is it appropriate to tell an associate that she has spinach in her teeth? True or False
8. If you need to excuse yourself during a meal, you place your napkin to the left of your place setting. True or False
9. BBQ ribs are a good meal option at a company banquet. True or False
10. Pushing back your plate signals you are finished eating. True or False

 Task Requirements

The students are divided into groups with 6 members each. Student A and D play the roles as the staff of International Sales Department of the company. Student B plays a role as the client from China. Student C plays a role as the manager of International Sales Department of the company. Student E plays a role as the CEO of the Company. Student F plays a role as the receptionist of the hotel.

---

1. Based on http://www.iiamd.org/Mess.Nov.Dec06.pdf, by Dr. Kathleen Pagana.

Task 1 Writing an Invitation Letter

An invitation letter is an invitation to a celebration, a special function, an open house, a company function, an introduction of a new product or program or a special offer. A formal invitation letter is used for the purpose of exchanges for business, sales, grants, delegations etc. The letter must contain the address of the inviter and the invitee as well. A business letter should clearly express the contact persons regarding the business deal and other important matters concerned. In short, the format must have a professional appeal. Also note that, it should have the logo of the company at its letterhead. Be sure your invitation letter includes: The name of the person sponsoring the event. Exactly who is invited. What type of social event is being held. The date, address, and time of the event Directions or preferred, the phone number and deadline to reply; precede these facts with "RSVP" (French abbreviation for "please reply").

Student C plays a role as Christine Winters, the manager of the International Sales Department of Rainbow Pet Products Co., Ltd., Los Angeles, California.

Christine Winters writes an invitation letter to Wang Fuguo, the Purchase Department Manager of Beijing Huacheng Pet Products Shops, 135 Chaoyang Street, Chaoyang District, Beijing 100026, China, who has placed a big order in Oct. with Rainbow Pet Products Co., Ltd., Los Angeles, California. She invites Wang Fuguo as Rainbow's valued client to attend the 20th Anniversary Celebration of Rainbow Pet Products Co., Ltd. on Monday, Jan. 7th, 2013 at Hilton Checkers Hotel Los Angeles, 535 South Grand Avenue, Los Angeles, California 90071. The program is as follows (Table 6-1).

Encl

Table 6-1
Rainbow Pet Products Co., Ltd., Los Angeles, California
The 20th Anniversary Celebration

Date Jan. 6-7th, 2013
Address: Hilton Checkers Hotel Los Angeles, 535 South Grand Avenue, Los Angeles

Date/Time	Activity
Jan. 6th, 2013	
8:00-18:00	Pickup Service at Los Angeles International Airport Check-in Service at Hilton Checkers Hotel Los Angeles
19:30-21:00	Welcome Dinner at Checkers Downtown Restaurant
Jan. 7th, 2013	
7:00-8:30	Standard English and Continental breakfasts (Free) at Hilton Checkers Hotel Los Angeles
8:30-9:00	Registration

Module Six *Customer Reception*

9:00 -11:30	The 20th Anniversary Celebration
12:00 -14:00	Buffet (Free) at Hilton Checkers Hotel Los Angeles
14:00-17:00	Factory Visit
19:30-21:00	Banquet at Hilton Checkers Hotel Los Angeles
Jan. 8th, 2013	
7:00-8:30	Standard English and Continental breakfasts (Free) at Hilton Checkers Hotel Los Angeles
8:00-18:00	Seeing Off Service at Los Angeles International Airport

Contact: Daniel Zheng
Tel: 213-345-9125
Fax: 213-345-9125
E-mail:danielzheng@yahoo.com

 Write an invitation letter with the following information according to the program (Table 6-1).
- Opening sentence
- Invite the receiver to the 20th anniversary celebration
- Ask for confirmation information such as arriving date, time, and flight number
- Enclosed the program
- Bring the invitation card
- Closing sentence

(150-200 words)

Rainbow Pet Products Co., Ltd., Los Angeles, California.
1358 Westwood Blvd
Los Angeles, CA90024-4911
USA

Tel: 213-345-9120
Fax: 213-345-9108
E-mail:christinewinters@yahoo.com

Dec 7th, 2012

Wang Fuguo

109

Purchase Department Manager
Beijing Huacheng Pet Products Shops
135 Chaoyang Street
Chaoyang District
Beijing 100026
China

Dear Mr. Wang:

Sincerely,
Rainbow Pet Products Co., Ltd., Los Angeles, California
Christine Winters
Christine Winters
Manager of International Sales Department

Encl: Program

 Fill in the invitation card with the following information according to the conference program.

- Guest's Name
- Venue
- Date
- Time

(No more than 20)

Rainbow Pet Products Co., Ltd., Los Angeles, California
The 20th Anniversary Celebration
Request the honor of _____ presence
at _____
on _____
from _____

Task 2 Accepting the Invitation

When writing an acceptance to the invitation, state you are accepting "the kind invitation of" the sender, and repeat the details about the day and time as a way for the hosts to confirm you have these details correct. And then tells him the detailed information needed.

Student B plays a role as Wang Fuguo, the Purchase Department Manager of Beijing Huacheng Pet Products Shops, 135 Chaoyang Street, Chaoyang District, Beijing 100026, China.

Wang Fuguo receives the invitation letter. He replies to accept the invitation. And he tells Christine Winters that he will arrive on Sunday, Jan. 6, 2013, at 5:00 p.m. on flight CA983.

 Write a letter with the following information.

- Opening sentence
- Accept the invitation
- Give the information such as arriving date, time, and flight number
- Closing sentence

(150-200 words)

Beijing Huacheng Pet Products Shops
135 Chaoyang Street
Chaoyang District
Beijing 100026
China

Tel: 010-8762-2367
Fax: 010-8762-2368
E-mail:wangfuguo@yahoo.com

Dec 14th, 2012

Christine Winters
Manager of the International Sales Department
Rainbow Pet Products Co., Ltd., Los Angeles, California.
1358 Westwood Blvd
Los Angeles, CA90024-4911
USA

Dear Mrs. Winters:

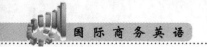

> Sincerely yours,
> Beijing Huacheng Pet Products Shops
> Wang Fuguo
> Wang Fuguo
> Purchase Department Manager

Task 3 Meeting at the Airport

If you're meeting someone at the airport, check the flight is on time before you leave. Information screens in the arrivals area display live flight status information.

The status message may be:

Expected: The flight hasn't landed yet.

Landed: The flight has arrived but passengers have yet to clear passport control and pick up baggage.

Baggage in hall: Passengers should be in the arrivals area shortly.

Student A plays a role as Daniel Zheng, the international salesperson of the International Sales Department of Rainbow Pet Products Co., Ltd., Los Angeles, California.

Student B plays a role as Wang Fuguo, the Purchase Department Manager of Beijing Huacheng Pet Products Shops, 135 Chaoyang Street, Chaoyang District, Beijing 100026, China.

Student F plays a role as Emily Pearls, the receptionist of Hilton Checkers Hotel Los Angeles.

Daniel Zheng gets the customer reception task from Christine Winters to pick Wang Fuguo up at the airport and take him to the hotel. Emily Pearls helps them to check in.

 Simulate the situation according to the above information.

Task 4 Having a Welcome Dinner

A Welcome Dinner is a large meal or feast which usually serves a purpose to welcome valued guests.

Student A plays a role as Daniel Zheng, the international salesperson of International Sales Department of Rainbow Pet Products Co., Ltd., Los Angeles, California.

Student B plays a role as Wang Fuguo, the Purchase Department Manager of Beijing Huacheng Pet Products Shops.

Student C plays a role as Christine Winters, the manager of International Sales Department of Rainbow Pet Products Co., Ltd., Los Angeles, California.

Student D plays a role as Andrew Hard, the director of the Asian section of the International Sales Department of Rainbow Pet Products Co., Ltd., Los Angeles, California.

Module Six *Customer Reception*

Student E plays a role as Doris Green, the CEO of Rainbow Pet Products Co., Ltd., Los Angeles, California.

Daniel Zheng represents Wang Fuguo to Christine Winters. Christine Winters introduces Andrew Hard to Wang Fuguo. And they greet each other, and then take seats. Doris Green makes a welcome toast to the guests.

 Simulate the situation according to the above information.

 Task 1 Writing an Invitation Letter

Rainbow Pet Products Co., Ltd., Los Angeles, California
1358 Westwood Blvd
Los Angeles, CA90024-4911
USA

Tel: 213-345-9120
Fax: 213-345-9120
E-mail:christinewinters@yahoo.com

Dec 7th, 2012
Wang Fuguo
Purchase Department Manager
Beijing Huacheng Pet Products Shops
135 Chaoyang Street
Chaoyang District
Beijing 100026
China

Dear Mr. Wang Fuguo:

Our records show that you have been a valued client of Rainbow Pet Products Co., Ltd. since this year. Thank you for your business with us.

113

And I'm glad to invite you to the 20th Anniversary Celebration of Rainbow Pet Products Co., Ltd., Los Angeles, California on Monday, Jan. 7th, 2013 at Hilton Checkers Hotel Los Angeles, 535 South Grand Avenue, Los Angeles, California 90071.

We are going to accommodate you for the duration of your stay in Hilton Checkers Hotel Los Angeles. We will reserve the hotel after your confirmation.

After booking your ticket, please send us the confirmation including your arriving date, time and flight number to us as soon as possible. So we can know when exactly you are arriving in order to pick you up at the airport. Daniel Zheng will be waiting at Arrival Exit with your name on our sign.

I have enclosed the program for your reference.

The 20th Anniversary Celebration is by invitation card only. Please bring the invitation card with you.

I look forward to seeing you at the welcome Dinner.

Sincerely yours,
Rainbow Pet Products Co., Ltd., Los Angeles, California
Christine Winters
Christine Winters
Manager of International Sales Department

Encl.: Program

Rainbow Pet Products Co., Ltd., Los Angeles, California
The 20th Anniversary Celebration
Request the honor of <u>Mr. Wang Fuguo</u> presence
at <u>Hilton Checkers Hotel Los Angeles</u>
on <u>Monday, Jan. 7th, 2013</u>
from <u>8:30a.m.-9:00p.m.</u>

Task 2 Accepting the Invitation

Beijing Huacheng Pet Products Shops
135 Chaoyang Street
Chaoyang District
Beijing 100026
China

Module Six *Customer Reception*

Tel: 010-8762-2367
Fax: 010-8762-2368
E-mail:wangfuguo@yahoo.com

Dec 14th, 2012

Christine Winters
Manager of International Sales Department
Rainbow Pet Products Co., Ltd., Los Angeles, California.
1358 Westwood Blvd
Los Angeles, CA90024-4911
USA

Dear Mrs. Winters:

Thank you for inviting me to your 20th Anniversary Celebration on Monday, Jan. 6-7th, 2013 at Hilton Checkers Hotel Los Angeles, 535 South Grand Avenue, Los Angeles, California 90071. It's my pleasure to accept your invitation.

I'll be arriving on Sunday, Jan. 6th, 2013, at 5:00 p.m. on flight CA983 at Los Angeles International Airport. Thank you for offering to pick me up and getting me a room at Hilton Checkers Hotel Los Angeles. You seem to think of everything.

I look forward to meeting you.

Sincerely yours,
Beijing Huacheng Pet Products Shops
Wang Fuguo
Wang Fuguo
Purchase Department Manager

Task 3 Meeting at the Airport

(At the airport)
Daniel Zheng: Excuse me, Sir. Are you Mr. Wang from Beijing?
Wang Fuguo: Yes, I'm Wang Fuguo from Beijing Huacheng Pet Products Shops.
Daniel Zheng: I'm Daniel Zheng, from Rainbow Pet Products Co., Ltd., Los Angeles, California. I've come to meet you. I will accompany you during your stay here.
Wang Fuguo: Nice to meet you.
Daniel Zheng: Welcome to Los Angeles, Mr, Wang. Our manager, Mrs. Winters will come to greet you later at the Welcome Dinner. How was your flight?

Wang Fuguo: Great, I enjoyed it very much.

Daniel Zheng: Anyhow, it's a long way to Los Angeles, isn't it? I think you must be very tired.

Wang Fuguo: Yes, a little.

Daniel Zheng: How many pieces of Luggage do you have?

Wang Fuguo: Two pieces, they are all here.

Daniel Zheng: If all is ready, we'd better start for the hotel. Let me help you with your luggage.

Wang Fuguo: OK, thank you. It's a little heavy.

Daniel Zheng: Let's go to the parking lot directly, because it is not convenient here.

Wang Fuguo: That's OK.

Daniel Zheng: This way please.

(At the hotel)

Emily Pearls: Good afternoon. Welcome to Hilton Checkers Hotel Los Angeles. May I help you?

Daniel Zheng: Yes, I'd like to check-in, please. I'm Daniel Zheng. I have made a reservation for Mr. Wang Fuguo.

Emily Pearls: Just a moment please. I'll check our reservation record. (After a while) Thank you for waiting, Mr. Zheng. Your reservation is for a Business Suite from Jan. 6th to 7th for two nights prepaid. Is that right?

Daniel Zheng: Exactly.

Emily Pearls: Could you fill out the registration form, please?

Daniel Zheng: Fine, Mr. Wang, would you like to fill it in?

Wang Fuguo: That's OK. Here you are.

Emily Pearls: May I see your passport, please?

Wang Fuguo: Sure, here you are.

Emily Pearls: Thank you, Mr. Wang. Your room number is 4675. That's on the 4th floor. A bellman will show you the room. Please enjoy your stay.

Wang Fuguo: Thank you.

Daniel Zheng: I will pick you up at 7:20 p.m. to the welcome Dinner.

Wang Fuguo: I see, I will wait for you on time.

Daniel Zheng: Mr. Wang you'd better have a rest upstairs. See you then.

Wang Fuguo: See you later. Thanks for your help.

Daniel Zheng: My pleasure.

Task 4 Having a Welcome Dinner

Daniel Zheng: Mr. Wang, I'd like you to meet Mrs. Winters, our Sales Department Manager.

Wang Fuguo: I'd like to.

Daniel Zheng: Mr. Winters, this is Mr. Wang Fuguo, the Purchase Department Manager of Beijing Huacheng Pet Products Shops.

Christine Winters: Mr. Wang, nice to see you.

Wang Fuguo: Mrs. Winters, nice to see you. Thank you for your invitation.

Christine Winters: Welcome to Los Angeles, Mr. Wang. Have you ever met Andrew Hard? Andrew, you must be eager to meet Mr. Wang.

Andrew Hard: Mr. Wang, it's very nice to finally meet you, after so many phone calls and faxes.

Wang Fuguo: Me too. I have had a satisfied cooperation with you.

Andrew Hard: Thanks for your confidence, Mr. Wang.

Christine Winters: You'll find Andrew is a force to be reckoned with at Rainbow.

Wang Fuguo: He appears to be a talent with enthusiasm.

Christine Winters: Mr. Wang, you're the guest of honor, have a seat please.

Wang Fuguo: Lady first.

Christine Winters: Thank you.

Doris Green: Distinguished Guests, Ladies and Gentlemen, Dear Friends, the 20th Anniversary Celebration of Rainbow Pet Products Co., Ltd., Los Angeles, California will be held this evening. On behalf of all the staff of Rainbow, I wish to extend a warm welcome to all the distinguished guests who have come to Los Angeles for this event. I would like to express my sincere thanks to clients and customers for the sincere help and strong support they have given to the Rainbow. My thanks also go to all the friends for sincere friendship, and cooperation. Enjoy your dinner and have a good time tonight. Cheers!

All: Cheers!

Knowledges

Culture

Culture is the deposit of knowledge, experience, beliefs, values, actions, attitudes, hierarchies, religions, notions of time, roles, spatial relations, concepts of the universe and artifacts acquired by a group of people in the course of generations through individual and group striving.

Practice: True or False

1. Culture is the systems of knowledge shared by two people.

2. A culture is a way of life of a group of people—the behaviors, beliefs, values, and symbols that they accept, generally without thinking about them, and that are passed along by

communication and imitation from one generation to the next.

3. Culture in its broadest sense is cultivated behavior; that is the totality of a person's learned, accumulated experience which is socially transmitted, or more briefly, behavior through social learning.

4. Culture is symbolic communication. Some of its symbols include a group's skills, knowledge, attitudes, values, and motives.

5. Culture is a collective programming of the mind that distinguishes one from another.

6. Culture is learned, dynamic, pervasive, integrated and adaptive.

7. The essential core of culture is religion.

8. Culture is the sum of total of the learned behavior of a group of people that are generally considered to be the tradition of that people and are transmitted from generation to generation.

Business Etiquettes

Business Etiquettes are the expected behaviors and expectations for individual actions within society, group, or class. Within a place of business, it involves treating coworkers and employer with respect and courtesy in a way that creates a pleasant work environment for everyone.

Practice : Choose the best answer.

1. You're in a restaurant and a thin soup is served in a cup with no handles. To eat it you should:

   A. pick it up and drink it

   B. use the spoon provided

   C. eat half of it with a spoon and drink the remainder

2. You're at a dinner and champagne is served with the dessert. You simply can't drink champagne yet know the host will be offering a toast. Do you:

   A. tell the waiter "no champagne"?

   B. turn over your glass?

   C. ask the waiter to pour water into your champagne glass instead?

   D. say nothing and allow the champagne to be poured?

3. You're at a table in a restaurant for a business dinner. Midway through the meal, you're called to the telephone. What do you do with your napkin?

   A. Take it with you

   B. Fold and place it to the left of your plate

   C. Loosely fold it and place it on the right side

   D. Leave it on your chair

4. You're talking with a group of four people. Do you make eye contact with:

   A. just the person to whom you're speaking at the moment?

Module Six Customer Reception

B. each of the four, moving your eye contact from one to another?

C. no one particular person (not looking directly into anyone's eyes)?

5. You've forgotten a lunch with a business associate. You feel terrible and know he's furious. Do you:

A. write a letter of apology?

B. send flowers?

C. keep quiet and hope he forgets about it?

D. Call to apologize and set up another appointment?

 Skills Requirements

Vocabulary: Gesture

 Fill in column II with the meaning of the gesture

I	II
1. The thumb-up sign	
2. The thumb-down sign	
3. The "V" sign	
4. The single finger beckon	

Listening: Dinner Etiquette

 Listen to each sentence twice. Fill in Column II with A-I.

I	II
Do	
Don't	

Speaking: Invitation

Work in pairs with a partner. Look at the question. Take one minute to prepare your answer. Think of reasons to explain your choice. Then tell your partner your answer and reasons.

WHAT IS IMPORTANT WHEN …?
Having an invitation

- Dress for Invitation
- Be Punctual
- Express thanks to the host and hostess

Reading: Apple Stock Up on Positive Early Reviews for iPhone 5

 Read the passages below. Choose the best answers.

Apple Stock Up on Positive Early Reviews for iPhone 5

Thu, Sept. 13, 2012
By PATRICK SEITZPATRICK
INVESTOR'S BUSINESS DAILY

 Apple (AAPL) shares were up more than 1% in midday trading Thursday, a day after the consumer electronics giant showed off its fall product lineup, including the redesigned iPhone 5 and colorful new iPod music players.
 On Wednesday, Apple tacked on a 1.4% gain. Its shares are trading near 678, just below the all-time high of 683.29 reached on Monday.
 Investors showed confidence that Apple's new products will help drive sales to new heights.
 View Enlarged Image
 Analysts were uniformly positive on Apple's announcements, even though media leaks kept the surprises to a minimum. As expected, Apple launched its sixth-generation smartphone, the iPhone 5, which features a larger display, faster processor, 4G LTE wireless connectivity and improved camera in a thinner, lighter device. It also unveiled a new iPod Nano and iPod Touch lineup in bold colors and enhanced specs.
 "With Apple planning an aggressive iPhone 5 launch at 240 carriers in 100 countries by year end, we remain confident in our above-consensus December quarter iPhone estimates," Canaccord Genuity analyst Michael Walkley said in a research note Thursday. "We believe Apple's industry-leading software ecosystem and leading hardware expertise will lead to a strong multiyear product cycle."
 Walkley has a buy rating on the stock, with a price target of 797.
 "We believe Apple is well positioned for very strong (fiscal year) 2013 sales and earnings growth driven by new product introductions, including the recently refreshed MacBook Air and Pro series, iPod lineup, LTE iPhone 5 and potentially iPad Mini and iTV in the coming months," he said.

Module Six *Customer Reception*

Janney Capital Markets analyst Bill Choi raised his Q4 sales estimates for Apple based on what he heard at the event.

"The event was largely in line with our expectations, and we believe the new iPhone 5 form factor will help drive a strong upgrade cycle," he wrote in a report Thursday. "IPhone 5 availability and international roll-out schedule leaves us incrementally more positive on any rumored supply constraints and reaffirms our view that there may be room for upside to current Q4 estimates."

Despite the recent run-up in Apple's stock price, Choi sees room for further appreciation based on pent-up demand and a strong international rollout for the iPhone 5 — and the potential for new products like the iPad Mini tablet and iTV television.

Choi has a buy rating on Apple, with a target of 720.

RBC Capital Markets analyst Amit Daryanani raised his price target on Apple to 750 from 700 after the Wednesday event. He rates the stock outperform.

Daryanani attended the event and "walked away impressed with the new smartphone," which goes on sale Sept. 21, he wrote in a research note Thursday. It should provide a leg up on competitors using Google's (GOOG) Android operating system, including Samsung, he said.

The iPhone 5 is "a material upgrade from past iterations that should drive a material upgrade cycle," Daryanani said. He estimates that Apple could ship 8 million to 10 million units in the September quarter and 50 million units or more in the December and March quarters.

"We believe the iPhone 5 could be the biggest upgrade in the company's history," Daryanani said.

ISI analyst Brian Marshall spent some time with the iPhone 5 on Thursday and came away "thoroughly impressed," he said in a report Wednesday. "Its complete redesign and the feature list did not disappoint," he said.

William Blair analyst Anil Doradla was less impressed with Apple's announcements. The iPhone 5 was in line with expectations, but there was no "wow factor," he wrote in a report late Wednesday. Doradla, though, also rates the stock outperform.

Apple might not be done with its fall product launch announcements yet. Analysts expect the company to announce the iPad Mini in October.

1. When was the Apple iPhone 5 launched?
   A. Tuesday   B. Wednesday   C. Thursday

2. Which one is wrong?
   A. The iPhone 5 is the fifth generation smartphone.
   B. The iPhone 5 has a larger display.
   C. The iPhone 5 becomes thinner and lighter.

3. Which one has not been launched yet?
   A. iTV   B. iPod Touch   C. iPhone 5

4. Which one is wrong?
   A. William Blair is totally satisfied with iphone 5.
   B. Brian Marshall is thoroughly impressed by iPnone 5.
   C. Daryanani believes iPhone 5 could be the biggest upgrade.

5. When will the iPad Mini be launched?
   A. September   B. October   C. November

Writing: Invitation Card

 Write an invitation card according to the following information.
- Inviter: Mr. and Mrs. James Stanley
- Time: 7:30 p.m., Sunday, Jan. 20th, 2013
- Site: Kowloon Shangri-la Hotel, 64 Mody Road, Tsimshatsui East, Kowloon, Hongkong
- Activity: Welcome Dinner

(no more than 50)

Business Negotiation

导入案例

你是什么类型的谈判者？

任务要求

学生分成三人一组，分别扮演新员工及其主管和客户，进行贸易磋商。

任务流程

1. 新员工和客户在展会上首次接触。
2. 新员工陪客户参观工厂。
3. 新员工及其主管与客户进行商务谈判。
4. 客户下订单。

知识要点

1. 国际商务谈判。
2. 国际商务谈判的基本类型。

技能要求

1. 词汇：国际贸易术语。
2. 听：国际商务谈判。
3. 说：催开信用证。
4. 读：谈判不仅仅是谈价格。
5. 写：拒绝订单。

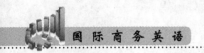

 Leading In

Which kind of negotiator are you? [1]

True or False.

1. Negotiating is concerned with winning more points than the other side.

2. If the other party is a hard, aggressive negotiator, then we must use the same tactics in self-defense.

3. If our organization is large, we should be prepared to use our power to influence the outcome.

4. Negotiation is about concluding a contract.

5. It is a sign of weakness to be slow and cautious in reaching agreement.

6. People who are demanding and uncompromising make the best negotiators.

7. There is nothing wrong with giving misleading information if it is going to help you get what you want from negotiations.

8. It is dangerous to allow the other party to know what you really want in a negotiation.

9. We have failed in a negotiation if we do not get exactly what we want.

10. There can only be one winner in any negotiation.

 Task Requirements

The students are divided into groups with 3 members each. Student A plays a role as the new staff. Student B plays a role as the client. Student C plays a role as the director of the new staff.

Task 1 Touching in the Fair

A fair is a gathering of people to display or trade produce or other goods. It is normally of the essence of a fair that it is temporary; some last only an afternoon while others may last as long as ten weeks. Activities at fairs vary widely. Some trade fairs are important regular business events where either products are traded between business people, or where products are showcased to largely consumer attendees. It is a good opportunity for the first touch of buyers and sellers.

Student A plays a role as Daniel Zheng, the international salesperson of the International Sales Department of Rainbow Pet Products Co., Ltd., Los Angeles, California.

Student B plays a role as Zhang Hongsheng, the trade representative of Beijing Hongda Pet

---

1. based on http://www.totalsuccess.co.uk/negotiating-with-difficult-people/ by admin on July 17, 2011.

Module Seven *Business Negotiation*

Products Shops.

Zhang Hongsheng is interested in the Rainbow Pet Products displayed at the 6th Pet Products Spring Fair, Los Angeles. He asks Daniel Zheng for detailed information at the booth. And they decide to visit the Rainbow plants right now.

Simulate the situation according to the above information.

Task 2 Visiting the Plant

Visiting the plants is essential for the customer to understand the commodity. The factory equipment, scale and the quality of workers and the decision maker's management ability determines the quality of the product. It is a necessary steps for the purchaser to make decisions. It is of great significance to have the direct and objective understanding of the production.

Student A plays a role as Daniel Zheng, the international salesperson of the International Sales Department of Rainbow Pet Products Co., Ltd., Los Angeles, California.

Student B plays a role as Zhang Hongsheng, the trade representative of Beijing Hongda Pet Products Shops.

Zhang Hongsheng visits the plant of Rainbow Pet Products Co., Ltd., Los Angeles, California with the company of Daniel Zheng. And he is satisfied with the nutrition products. He makes an enquiry for Milk Replacer. But he thinks the prices in the price list are too high. And he decides to make further negotiation after he flies back from New York.

Simulate the situation according to the above information.

Task 3 Having a Business Negotiation

During the negotiation, many issues should be talked about by the sellers and the buyers. They are quality, quantity and packing of the goods, price, shipment, insurance, payment terms, commodity inspection, disputes and settlement of disputes, force majeure, and arbitration, etc..

Student A plays a role as Daniel Zheng, the international salesperson of the International Sales Department of Rainbow Pet Products Co., Ltd., Los Angeles, California.

Student B plays a role as Zhang Hongsheng, the trade representative of Beijing Hongda Pet Products Shops.

Student C plays a role as Andrew Hard, the director of the Asian section of the International Sales Department of Rainbow Pet Products Co., Ltd., Los Angeles, California.

Zhang Hongsheng comes back from New York. Daniel Zheng and Zhang Hongsheng have a business negotiation for the first round. Zhang Hongsheng is not satisfied with the price on the price list as follows (Table 7-1). Daniel Zheng gives 10 percent discount. But Zhang Hongsheng wants 30 percent discount. Daniel Zheng asks Andrew Hard. Andrew Hard gives 15 percent discount. And after several rounds of negotiation. They make a deal at 22 percent allowance according to the price list. Packing should be in wooden cases of 20 boxes each. The Insurance should be covered by the sellers for 110% of the invoice value against WPA. The goods should be delivered within a month after receiving the order and paid by D/P sight.

Table 7-1 Price List

Price List Rainbow Pet Products Co., Ltd., Los Angeles, California					
Dog Products Rainbow has multiple solutions for your dog's health needs.					
Catogaries	Item No.	Title	Description	Price USD CIF Tianjin	
Milk Replacer	DM-101	Milk Replacer for Dogs	Enriched with Colostrum Food Supplement for Puppies & Pregnant or Lactating Dogs Net Wt. 12 Oz. per box	16.00	
	DM-102	Milk Replacer for Dogs (Lg)	Enriched with Colostrum Food Supplement for Puppies & Pregnant or Lactating Dogs Net Wt. 28 Oz. per box	38.00	
Cat Products Rainbow has multiple solutions for your cat's health needs.					
Catogaries	Item No.	Title	Description	Remarks	
Milk Replacer	CM-101	Milk Replacer for Cats Enriched with Colostrum	Food Supplement for Kittens & Pregnant or Lactating Cats Net Wt. 12 Oz. per box	12.00	
Milk Replacer	CM-102	Milk Replacer for Cats	Enriched with Colostrum Food Supplement for Kittens & Pregnant or Lactating Cats Net Wt. 6 Oz. per box	5.00	

 Simulate the situation according to the above information.

Task 4 Placing an Order

An order is a confirmed request by one party to another to buy, sell, deliver, or receive goods or services under specified terms and conditions. When accepted by the receiving party, an order becomes a legally binding contract.

Student B plays a role as Zhang Hongsheng, the trade representative of Beijing Hongda Pet Products Shops.

Zhang Hongsheng places an order according to the terms discussed in Task 3(7.2.3).

Module Seven *Business Negotiation*

 Place an order with the following information.
- Commodity
- Quality
- Quantity
- Date of shipment
- Packing
- Terms of Payment
- Insurance

BEIJING HONGDA PET PRODUCTS SHOP

356 Chaoyang Street   Tel: +86-(0)10-6738-3027
Chaoyang District   Fax: +86-(0)10-6738-3027
Beijing 100026
China

May 1st, 2013

Order No. 4756
Daniel Zheng
International Sales Department
Rainbow Pet Products Co., Ltd., Los Angeles, California.
1358 Westwood Blvd
Los Angeles, CA90024-4911
USA

Dear Mr. Zheng:

Sincerely yours,
Hongda Pet Products Shops
Zhang Hongsheng
Zhang Hongsheng
Trade Representative

 Task Process

Task 1 Touching in the Fair

Daniel Zheng: Good morning, sir. Can I help you?
Zhang Hongsheng: Yes. I'm Zhang Hongsheng, the trade representative of Beijing Hongda

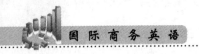

Pet Products Shops.

Daniel Zheng: Nice to meet you, Mr. Zhang. I'm Daniel Zheng, the international salesperson of Rainbow Pet Products Co., Ltd., Los Angeles, California. Here is my name card.

Zhang Hongsheng: Thank you, Mr. Zheng. Here is my card.

Daniel Zheng: Thank you.

Zhang Hongsheng: I'm interested in your Pet Products on display. Would you like to give me some detailed information about your products?

Daniel Zheng: Of course. Here are the catalogs of all lines of our products. There are two major categories of products in our company. One is professional Pet Nutrition such as Multivitamins and Milk Replacer. The other is Pet Supplies such as pet beds, pet clothes and pet toys. Which kinds of products are you interested in?

Zhang Hongsheng: Our company is one of the big dealers of Pet Products in China. I'm interested in all kinds of Pet Products which can attract the Pet Owners. And I'd like to learn more about your products. Will you give me more samples of each line of your products? If I am satisfied with your samples, we could have a good business relationship.

Daniel Zheng: I'd like to enter into business relations with you too. Would you like to visit our plant so we can show you the samples and what we can do for you. You will surely know the products better after the visit. When would it be a good time for you, today or tomorrow?

Zhang Hongsheng: I will fly to New York tomorrow to have a negotiation with a provider. So, is it convenient for you to show me around now?

Daniel Zheng: Of course. Let's go to the parking lot. I'll drive you to our plant. This way please.

Task 2 Visiting the Plant

Daniel Zhen: I'll show you around and explain our products as we go along.

Zhang Hongsheng: That'll be most helpful. What's that building opposite us?

Daniel Zheng: That is our office block. We have all the administrative departments there. The Product Department and Logistic Department are both on the first floor. The Customer Service Department and the R&D Department are on the second floor. Our department is on the third floor.

Zhang Hongsheng: How about that one?

Daniel Zheng: Down there is the nutrition products plant. Would you like to go there first?

Zhang Hongsheng: Sure. When was the plant set up?

Daniel Zheng: It is originally founded in 1993. And we have celebrated our 20th anniversary in January this year. Our company is to be recognized as one of the leaders in the Pet Products industry.

Zhang Hongsheng: Congratulations!

Daneil Zheng: Thank you. Would you like to put on the hooded jumpsuit and wash hands thoroughly, visitors should walk through a pool of disinfectant and then into the plant in order to keep abreast of health and safety for the production.

Zhang Hongsheng: Of course. That's necessary. How do you control the quality?

Daniel Zheng: All products have to go through five checks in the whole manufacturing process.

Zhang Hongsheng: What's your best selling line?

Daniel Zheng: We are famous for the Pet Nutrition, because the Rainbow science and research team take the lead in pet nutrition solutions for cats and dogs. The Nutrition Products are best selling line. There are two main kinds of nutrition products, Multivitamins and Milk Replacers. The Multivitamins are mature products in the product life cycle. But the Milk Replacers are the star product of our company backed by high quality, market longevity, and good support. Milk Replacers provide the nutrients necessary for a thriving, healthy young puppy or kitten. This is the sample of the Milk Replacers for puppies. This is our latest product and it's totally on our own. We are strongly recommending this product for its good quality. There's a great demand for this.

Zhang Hongsheng: That's wonderful. Do you have any more detailed printed material on this product?

Daniel Zheng: Here are the brochures you asked for. And we have pamphlets in Chinese too.

Zhang Hongsheng: I'd like to take these brochures with me. And I want these price lists as well.

Daniel Zheng: Go right ahead. Please take whatever you like.

Zhang Hongsheng: Could I have this sample free of charge?

Daniel Zheng: Yes, of course. But you should sign here.

Zhang Hongsheng: That's OK. I was so impressed by the good quality of your Products. But your price looks too high.

Daniel Zheng: You'll find our products are worth the price.

Zhang Hongsheng: I'd like to have a further negotiation with you after I am back from New York. Thank you. You are so helpful.

Daniel Zheng: We hope you enjoyed the visit to our plant. When would you be back?

Zhang Hongsheng: I'll be back on 26th April. How about 14:00 in the afternoon?

Daniel Zheng: That's OK.

Zhang Hongsheng: It was very kind of you to give me a tour of the place. It gave me a good idea of your product range.

Daniel Zheng: It's a pleasure to show our plant to our customers.

Task 3 Having a Business Negotiation

(Round 1)

Daniel Zheng: I'm glad that you could be here today, Mr. Zhang. How about your trip.

Zhang Hongsheng: Great. I have made a big deal with the dealers in New York. And I hope to establish business relations with you.

Daniel Zheng: After examing our products, what are you interested in?

Zhang Hongsheng: Of course your star products. The Milk Replacer DM-101 and CM-101. If your price is acceptable, I'd like to place a great order with you. But the price on your price list is rather high.

Daniel Zheng: As you know, there are drops in prices with volume increase.

Zhang Hongsheng: I'd like to place an order of 40,000 boxes each items, which will be followed by big orders if our clients are satisfied with your quality and price.

Daniel Zheng: If you order more than 50,000 boxes each item, we will give you ten percent discount.

Zhang Hongsheng: I don't think we'll be able to pay these prices. As you know, the providers in New York offered us a price 30% lower than yours.

Daniel Zheng: When you compare the prices, you must take everything into consideration. Our products are of high quality. Comparing with other goods of similar quality, I'm sure you'll find that our prices are reasonable and very competitive.

Zhang Hongsheng: I'm afraid I can't agree with you there. I grant that yours are of better quality, But the gap is too wide if comparing with other supplier's price

Daniel Zheng: I'll check back with my boss for you. We may be able to work out a better deal for you. Would you like to have a cup of coffee.

Zhang Hongsheng: OK, I'm waiting for you.

(Round 2)

Daniel Zheng: I have checked with my boss, he agreed to give you 15% allowance if you ordered more than 50,000 boxes each item. Actually that's about the best we can do on that.

Zhang Hongsheng: It seems to me that it's still rather high.

Daniel Zheng: This is a good chance of reducing them by 15%. We haven't given a favorable price like that.

Zhang Hongsheng: If I ordered 80,000 boxes, how much do you think you could bring the price down?

Daniel Zheng: This is the lowest possible price.

Zhang Hongsheng: Then, thank you for your reception. It seems to me that I have to place the order with New York.

Daniel Zheng: Can you wait a minute?

Module Seven *Business Negotiation*

(Round 3)

Daniel Zheng: Mr. Zhang, this is our director, Andrew Hard. Mr. Hard, this is Mr. Zhang.

Andrew Hard: Nice to see you, Mr. Zhang.

Zhang Hongsheng: Nice to see you, Mr. Hard.

Andrew Hard: I have heard of that you have visited our plant?

Zhang Hongsheng: Yes.

Andrew Hard: What's your general impression, may I ask?

Zhang Hongsheng: Very impressive, indeed, especially quality control system.

Andrew Hard: That's why our products are favorable in the world. OK, let's get down to business now. Are these new prices acceptable for you?

Zhang Hongsheng: We have to work out the final price. But your price is rather high for me. If you are going to occupy the Chinese market, your price should be attractive to Chinese customers.

Andrew Hard: Then how much do you want to pay?

Zhang Hongsheng: How about giving me 25% allowance if we order 80,000 boxes each item.

Andrew Hard: I'll give you 20% if you order 80,000 boxes each item, and 22% allowance if you order 100,000 boxes each item. I'm afraid that there is no room to negotiate the price.

Zhang Hongsheng: If I placed an order now, how long would it be before I got delivery?

Andrew Hard: It would largely depend on the size of the order and the items you want.

Zhang Hongsheng: 100,000 boxes DM-101 and 100,000 boxes CM101.

Andrew Hard: It will be delivered in three months after we receive your order.

Zhang Hongsheng: If you could deliver in one month and paid by D/P 60 day's sight, I'd like to accept 22% allowance.

Andrew Hard: One month is OK. But for payment, we usually require 100% value, confirmed, and irrevocable letter of credit in our favor, payable (available) by draft at sight.

Zhang Hongsheng: You must be aware that when we open a letter of credit, we have to pay a deposit and there will be bank charges in connection with the establishment of a letter of credit.

Andrew Hard: You know, Mr. Smith. An irrevocable letter of credit gives both the exporter and importer the additional protection of the banker's guarantee.

Zhang Hongsheng: That will tie up my funds and add to the cost of my imports.

Andrew Hard: How about meeting each other halfway? We can accept D/P sight as an exception.

Zhang Hongsheng: That's great. Well, we've settled the questions of price, quality, quantity, date of shipment, terms of payment. Now what about the packing, and insurance?

Andrew Hard: Very well. You know, The goods are to be packed in wooden cases of 20 boxes each.

Zhang Hongsheng: Good. The outer packing should be strong enough for transportation.

Andrew Hard: You may rest assured that the packing is strong enough to withstand rough handling.

Zhang Hongsheng: We need our order number on the outside of each wooden case. It makes it easier for us when we get the order on the dock.

Daniel Zheng: That will be no problem. We'll take care of it for you.

Zhang Hongsheng: One more thing. I think we need to discuss the terms of insurance.

Andrew Hard: You know, we generally insure WPA on a CIF offer.

Zhang Hongsheng: That's OK. Make a deal?

Andrew Hard: Deal.

Zhang Hongsheng: I'll place an order with you when I get back Beijing.

Andrew Hard: That's great. And Daniel Zheng will be responsible for your order. And don't hesitate to contact him as soon as you need any help.

Zhang Hongsheng: Thank you very much.

Task 4 Placing an Order

BEIJING HONGDA PET PRODUCTS SHOP

356 Chaoyang Street   Tel: +86-(0)10-6738-3027
Chaoyang District   Fax: +86-(0)10-6738-3027
Beijing 100026
China

May 1st, 2013

Order No. 4756

Daniel Zheng
International Sales Department
Rainbow Pet Products Co., Ltd., Los Angeles, California.
1358 Westwood Blvd
Los Angeles, CA90024-4911
USA

Dear Mr. Zheng,

Re: Milk Replacer

I appreciate your reception in Los Angeles.
I'm pleased to give you an initial order for the following items.

Item No.	Title	Description	Quantity (boxes)	Unit Price USD CIF Tianjin
DM-101	Milk Replacer for Dogs	Enriched with Colostrum Food Supplement for Puppies & Pregnant or Lactating Dogs Net Wt. 12 Oz. per box	100,000	12.48
CM-101	Milk Replacer for Cats Enriched with Colostrum	Food Supplement for Kittens & Pregnant or Lactating Cats Net Wt. 12 Oz. per box	100,000	9.36
Total Price			200,000	2184,000

Packing: In wooden cases of 20 boxes each.
Insurance: To be covered by the sellers for 110% of the invoice value against WPA.
Port of shipment: Los Angeles, USA
Port of destination: Tianjin, China
Shipping mark: At sellers' option
Time of shipment: On June 1st, 2013, transshipment and partial shipment not allowed.
Terms of Payment: By D/P sight.
We expect to find a good market for the above and hope to place further and larger orders with you in the near future.
Please send us your confirmation of sales in duplicate.

Sincerely yours,
Beijing Hongda Pet Products Shops
Zhang Hongsheng
Zhang Hongsheng
Trade Representative

International Business Negotiation

Negotiation is a process of communication between parties to manage conflicts in order for them to come to an agreement, solve a problem or make arrangements.

Business negotiation (BN) is a process of negotiating on business terms and coming to an agreement at the end between different business parties in pursuit of their respective economic benefits.

International Business Negotiation (IBN) is a process of information exchanging, talking and discussing, aiming at coming to an agreement in order to satisfy certain demand(s) of participants from different nations or regions in international business.

Practice: True or False

1. Negotiation involves exchange of ideas, communication, persuasion, compromise, and suchlike.
2. The objective of a negotiation could be definite or indefinite.
3. Negotiation must be built on the basis of mutual concession.
4. Every negotiation involves only two parties.
5. Negotiation must be conducted on an equal basis.
6. The objective of business negotiation is to obtain financial interest.
7. The core of negotiation is price.
8. The principle of business negotiation should be equality and mutual benefit.
9. Items of contract should keep strictly accurate.
10. International political factors must be taken into account in international business negotiation.

Basic Forms of International Business Negotiation

Classification by procedure

Horizontal Negotiation is the conferring process in which all the issues concerned are presented first and then discussed one by one, and an issue which cannot be settled at once may be skipped and settled later until all the issues are settled properly.

Vertical Negotiation is the haggling process in which all the issues to be discussed are listed according to their logical relations and then settled one by one in this logical order.

Classification by Site

Host-Court negotiation is the negotiation happened at the place where we are based or at our home court.

Guest-Court negotiation is the negotiation held at the location of the counterpart.

Third-place negotiation is the location held at a third-place. There is neither a host court nor a guest. It is a location in a neutral country or a neutral area.

Classification by Method

Oral negotiation refers to the situation in which the negotiators from each side talk with each other face to face or over the phone.

Written negotiation refers to the situation in which the participants in the negotiation confer contractual clauses by means of letters, telegraphs, faxes, e-mails and other written forms.

Classification by Participating Parties

One-to-one negotiation refers to the situation in which each buyer or seller, or each party in the proposed cooperation project entrusts only one negotiator from each side to confer face-to-face and one-to-one on its behalf.

Team negotiation is the one in which a negotiation team is constructed by each side to participate on behalf of its organization.

Module Seven Business Negotiation

Multilateral Negotiation is also dubbed as "multi-angles" negotiation, which refers to the business negotiating situation in which negotiators representing three or more interest groups from different countries confer to reach an agreement.

Practice: Fill A-L into Column II.

I	II Advantages
Host-court negotiation	
Guest-court negotiation	
Third-place negotiation	

A: The arrangement enables the home team to receive the direct instructions from their authority easily.

B: Choosing a place acceptable to both sides helps to build an objective and rational atmosphere for the negotiation.

C: It saves home team the traveling expenses abroad.

D: Traveling team can save the trouble to extend their hospitality.

E: Both sides attach great importance to their own image, reputation and etiquette.

F: Staying on the foreign land allows the guest to be free from distractions and concentrate on the negotiation.

G: Host team know the negotiation environment well and can be quite relaxed psychologically.

H: All the resources are readily available to the host negotiators.

I: When problems crop up, the traveling team has sound excuses or room to maneuver.

J: All negotiators are easily free from distractions.

K: If necessary, the guests may ask to negotiate directly with the supervisor of their rivalries.

L: The negotiation would not be delayed without an end, and at least both sides would like to see some progress big or small made in this round of negotiation.

Fill A-F into Column II.

I	II Disadvantages
Oral Negotiation	
Written Negotiation	

A. It tends to be simple and concise, and therefore sometimes it would lead to misunderstanding, resulting in disputes or conflicts.

B. There is a little room to maneuver. It is impossible to make a through consideration in a great hurry.

C. It is difficult to notice the changes in the counterpart's facial expression or psychology, which discourages the use of negotiating skills.

D. There is a heavier psychological pressure.

E. It is subject to the restriction of the communication facilities.

F. The atmosphere is widely changeable.

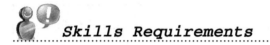

Vocabulary: Incoterms

 Fill in the blanks with "buyer" or "seller".

Incoterm	Loading on truck (carrier)	Export-Customs declare	Carriage to port of export	Unloading of truck in port of export	Loading charges in port of export	Carriage to port of import
EXW						
FCA						
FAS						
FOB						
CFR						
CIF						
DAT						
DAP						
CPT						
CIP						
DDP						

Incoterm	Unloading charges in port of import	Loading on truck in port of import	Carriage to place of destination	Insurance	Import customs clearance	Import taxes
EXW						
FCA						
FAS						
FOB						
CFR						
CIF						
DAT						
DAP						
CPT						
CIP						
DDP						

Module Seven Business Negotiation

Listening: Business Negotiation

 Listen to the dialogs twice. Choose the best answer according to what you have listened.

1. What happened to the goods?
   A. 30% cases are damaged
   B. 30% cartons are damaged
   C. 30% cartons are lost
2. Who will pay for the loss?
   A. The buyer   B. The Seller   C. Not mentioned
3. What is the price?
   A. USD120   B. USD127.5   C. USD135
4. Who will pay for the freight from Dalian to Qingdao?
   A. Mrs. Winters   B. Mr. Liu   C. Not mentioned
5. Which one can be accepted by Miss Bush?
   A. D/A   B. D/P   C. L/C

Speaking: Urging L/C

Suppose you are Mr. Ma. You are to make a phone call to Mr. Smith informing him that the shipment date is approaching but you haven't still received the relative L/C and urging him to expedite the L/C.

Reading: There's More to Negotiate than Just the Price

There's More to Negotiate than Just the Price[1]
By Barbara Taylor

When it comes to negotiating, it's easy to conjure up the old chess metaphor: a battle of wits, with one side out-strategizing the other to obtain victory. But when you're involved in negotiations every day, it feels more like a giant jigsaw puzzle — putting all the pieces on the table, staring down at them from different angles (sometimes for weeks on end), trying to identify the best fit.

It sometimes seems as if there are an infinite number of pieces in the puzzle and just as many ways for them to fit together. While we generally think of the purchase price and the 1. _____ payment as the key pieces, there are many others. My firm was involved in a recent negotiation in which the critical piece that made all the others fall into place had no monetary value whatsoever. It was simply a letter.

---

1. http://boss.blogs.nytimes.com/2009/12/21/theres-more-to-negotiate-than-just-the-price/.

Our client — I'll call her Debra — was the owner of a respected business that had been offering litigation-support services for almost 30 years. Her entrepreneurial route was familiar, starting with a home-based business that eventually grew into two offices covering eight counties and consistently grossing $2 million in annual 2. _____. After 3. _____ the business for sale nationwide, we ended up with three viable offers.

The first came in quickly from an out-of-state competitor. While there was no question that this buyer was qualified to purchase and operate the business, the terms of his initial offer were weak. The purchase price was barely half of Debra's asking price, and there were strings attached to her future employment at the company that didn't sit well. After several conversations, we made it clear that our client was not ready to accept and that we would continue to field other offers.

The next one came from a large regional firm looking to fill out its 4. _____ in the south-central United States. There was a flurry of excitement that we had received interest from such a prestigious acquirer. Initial talks went well. But as we started to negotiate, it became clear that we were dealing with "my way or the highway" thinking. We were told that the firm had completed 11 acquisitions in 10 years and that this was the way it did things. The 5. _____ of the offer would have left Debra with no money at closing and the entire purchase price paid out of gross monthly sales over a five-year period.

She had spent the better part of three decades building her business, and the thought of handing it over without putting a dime in her pocket was discouraging to say the least. She'd briefly had stars in her eyes at the thought of being part of such a big industry player, but she was turned off by its negotiating strategy, which was to not negotiate at all.

The third offer came from another highly qualified individual. He had run several companies like Debra's and was looking to relocate. He made a full-price 6. _____, but the down payment was about half of what Debra would have liked, and the payout of the remaining balance was tied to some aggressive annual sales targets. To muddy the waters further, the buyer was currently living in England, and he was unwilling to negotiate much. In the end, there appeared to be too many unknowns associated with his offer.

In the meantime, buyer No. 1 had been sweetening the pot. He submitted a second offer with a higher asking price, a higher down payment and fewer restrictions concerning Debra's role at the company. My husband, Chris, and I sensed we had a very interested buyer on the line, but Debra was still balking. We continued to shop the deal. A few weeks later, the buyer came back with another revision: 85 percent of Debra's original asking price with 60 percent down and a generous employment package. Bingo!

When Debra continued to waffle, we knew there was something other than money that was causing her to hesitate. After a candid chat, she told us that she had known the buyer for years and did not agree with some of his operating procedures. In fact, she thought they might even violate professional ethics. We immediately got everyone in a room for a face-to-face discussion. It all boiled down to one procedural technicality that 7. _____ from state to state. The buyer offered to pay for a legal opinion on the matter from a law firm of Debra's choosing. If the opinion letter came back favorable, she would accept the offer. Debra is scheduled to close on the sale of her business after the first of the year.

As Chris and I always say, every deal dies a thousand deaths. While strategy plays a part, a successful negotiation is frequently the result of patience, perseverance and creative problem 8. _____. If you keep working the puzzle long enough, things have a tendency to fall into place.

1. A. up   B. down   C. middle
2. A. revenue   B. cost   C. expend
3. A. selling   B. marketing   C. promoting
4. A. handprint   B. milestone   C. footprint
5. A. terms   B. contract   C. regulations

6. A. inquiry	B. offer	C. order
7. A. different	B. changed	C. varied
8. A. solved	B. to solve	C. solving

 Writing: Order

Reply the order below with the following information.

- Opening
- Express regret for not accepting
- Reasons
- Closing

(50-100 words)

From: stevenjones@yahoo.com
Date: Sept. 25th, 2013
To: xinhuatextiles@yahoo.com
Cc:
Subject: Order
Please supply:

Items	Commodity	Quality(pieces)	Unit Price(USD CIF New York)
A-389	Bed Sheets(120cm) Blue	5,000	US$15.00
B-287	Bed Sheets (106 cm) Green	4,000	US$12.00
Total Price		9,000	US$123,000

Best Regards
Steven Jones

From:
Date:
To:
Cc:
Subject:

Module Eight

Business Correspondence

导入案例

自我测试：三维贸易性格测试。

任务要求

学生分成二人一组，分别扮演新员工和客户，用英文商业信函完成贸易磋商，并签订合同。

任务流程

1. 新员工向潜在客户发促销信。
2. 客户进行询盘。
3. 新员工发出发盘。
4. 客户进行还盘。
5. 新员工接受还盘。
6. 双方签订合同。

知识要点

1. 国际贸易理论。
2. 全球化。

技能要求

1. 词汇：国际贸易组织。
2. 听：自由贸易区。
3. 说：贸易控制。
4. 读：国际贸易带来的好处。
5. 写：索赔理赔。

Module Eight *Business Correspondence*

 Leading In

Three Dimensions Trader Personality Quiz [1]

In order to make effective career decisions it is very important that you understand yourself. Knowing your strengths can be a difficult process and is essential if you are to be success in the graduate employment market. The following questions are designed to help you assess facts of your personality that are related to the kinds of trading approaches that are likely to work for you. There is no right or wrong answer. Rather, we are trying to find out your personal style, so that you can match it to your trading style. Each item consists of two statements. Please choose the statement that best describes you:

Part 1 measures a personality trait called "conscientiousness". A conscientious person is someone who has a high degree of self-control and perseverance.

---

1. A. I often arrive early for appointments and events to make sure I'm not late.
   B. I'm not very time-oriented and often show up late to appointments and events.
2. A. I tend to be detail-oriented and try to get each aspect of a job done as well as I can.
   B. I focus on the big picture instead of details and don't sweat the small aspects of a job.
3. A. I would be good at following a diet or exercise program.
   B. I would often cheat on a diet or exercise program.
4. A. I get routine maintenance done on my car when it is scheduled.
   B. I don't follow deadlines for routine maintenance on my car.

Part 2 measures a personality trait called "neuroticism". Neuroticism is the tendency to experience negative emotions.

---

1. A. When a problem occurs in my trading, I first feel frustrated and vent my feelings either outwardly or at myself.
   B. When a problem occurs in my trading, I first try to focus on what went wrong and what I can do to fix it.
2. A. If you could hear the thoughts in my head as I'm trading, you'd hear worried or negative thoughts.
   B. If you could hear the thoughts in my head as I'm trading, you'd hear me analyzing the market action.
3. A. It is hard for me to shake off setbacks in the market.
   B. I take market setbacks as a cost of doing business.
4. A. Sometimes I feel on top of the world in the market; other times, I'm down or down on myself.
   B. I don't have many emotional ups or downs in the market.
5. A. I trade by my gut.
   B. I trade with my head.

Part 3 measures a trader's risk aversion. A risk-averse trader is one who cannot tolerate the possibility of large losses and who would prefer smaller, more frequent wins with controlled losses to larger wins with greater drawdown.

---

1. Based on Three Dimensions (3D) Trader Personality Quiz (www.brettsteenbarger.com) by Brett N. Steenbarger, Ph.D..

1. A. When I go out to eat, I generally go to my favorite restaurants and order my favorite foods.
   B. When I go out to eat, I like to try new and unfamiliar restaurants and foods.
2. A. If I had a choice of car to drive, I would choose one that is comfortable and quiet.
   B. If I had a choice of car to drive, I would choose one that is fast and that handles well.
3. A. I like vacations that are peaceful and relaxing.
   B. I like vacations where you see and do a lot of different things.
4. A. I would like a job with a stable company that pays a guaranteed salary and benefits, even if I might not get rich.
   B. I would like a job with a startup company that offers me a chance to get rich, even if I might get laid off if things don't work out.
5. A. I try to eat healthy foods and get a good amount of exercise and rest.
   B. I'm very busy and don't always eat, exercise, and sleep as I should.
6. A. I avoid arguments and conflict.
   B. I like to argue and hash things out.

Test yourself

Part 1	1	2	3	4		
Part 2	1	2	3	4	5	
Part 3	1	2	3	4	5	6

Task Requirements

The students are divided into groups with 2 members each. Student A plays a role as the international salesperson. Student B plays a role as the client from China.

Task 1　Writing a Promotion Letter

A promotion letter is made to promote business or service to possible client. Normally, the letter is created to introduce products, items. The letter must be convincing so that the possible client will approve and accept the products being promoted.

Student A plays a role as Daniel Zheng, the salesperson of the International Sales Department of Rainbow Pet Products Co., Ltd., Los Angeles, California.

Daniel Zheng writes a promotion letter to Tianjin Shangwen Import and Export Corp., 46 Weijin Road, Nankai District, Tianjin 300071, China on Jan. 15th, 2013. He obtains the name and address from trade directory on the Internet. He encloses the catalogue as follows (Table 8-1).

Encl:

Table 8-1　Catalog

Catalog
Rainbow Pet Products Co., Ltd., Los Angeles, California

Module Eight *Business Correspondence*

Dog Products				
Rainbow has multiple solutions for your dog's health needs.				
Categories	Item No.	Title	Description	Remarks
Multivitamins	DV-101	Pet Chews™ PLUS D3 for Dogs	Maximum Daily Vitamin & Mineral Support for Dogs 60 Liver Flavored chewables	
	DV-102	Puppy Chews™	Complete Daily Multi-Vitamin & Mineral Supplement for Puppies 90 Liver Flavored Chewables	
Milk Replace	DM-101	Milk Replacer for Dogs	Enriched with Colostrum Food Supplement for Puppies & Pregnant or Lactating Dogs Net Wt. 12 Oz. per box	
	DM-102	Milk Replacer for Dogs (Lg)	Enriched with Colostrum Food Supplement for Puppies & Pregnant or Lactating Dogs Net Wt. 28 Oz. per box	
Cat Products				
Rainbow has multiple solutions for your cat's health needs.				
Categories	Item No.	Title	Description	Remarks
Multivitamins	CV-101	Pet Chews Calcium D3	Daily Calcium Supplement for Cats 180 Flavored Chewables	
	CV-102	Kitten Chews™	Complete Daily Multi-Vitamin & Mineral Supplement for Puppies 90 Liver Flavored Chewables	
Milk Replacer	CM-101	Milk Replacer for Cats Enriched with Colostrum	Food Supplement for Kittens & Pregnant or Lactating Cats Net Wt. 12 Oz. per box	
	CM-102	Milk Replacer for Cats	Enriched with Colostrum Food Supplement for Kittens & Pregnant or Lactating Cats Net Wt. 6 Oz. per box	

 Write a promotion letter with the following information.

- Opening sentence
- Be eager to establish relationship
- Brief introduction of the Pets Product
- Enclosed the catalog
- Closing sentence

(100-150 words)

Rainbow Pet Products Co., Ltd., Los Angeles, California.
1358 Westwood Blvd
Los Angeles, CA90024-4911
USA

Tel: 213-345-9125
Fax: 213-345-9125
E-mail:danielzheng@yahoo.com

Jan 15th, 2013

Import and Export Department
Tianjin Shangwen Import and Export Corp.
46 Weijin Road
Nankai District
Tianjin 300071
China

Gentlemen:

Re: "Rainbow" Brand Pet Products

Sincerely yours,
Rainbow Pet Products Co., Ltd., Los Angeles, California
Daniel Zheng
Daniel Zheng
International Sales Department

Encl: Catalog

Module Eight Business Correspondence

Task 2 Writing an Enquiry

Enquiry is a preliminary response from prospective customers, generally following an advertisement or sales promotion letter. It is also spelled as inquiry.

Student B plays a role as Guan Shan, the manager of Import and Export Department of Tianjin Shangwen Import and Export Corp.

Guan Shan writes an enquiry to Daniel Zheng on Jan. 20th, 2013, after receiving the promotion letter. And he is interested in Milk Replacers DM-101(10,000 boxes), DM-102(10, 000 boxes), CM-101(20, 000 boxes), CM-102(20,000 boxes) in the catalog. And he asks for an offer for the above Pet Products.

 Write an enquiry with the following information.
- Opening sentence
- Shows interest in specific products
- Asks for favorable price
- Closing sentence

(100-150 words)

Tianjin Shangwen Import and Export Corp.
46 Weijin Road
Nankai District
Tianjin 300071
China

Tel: 022-2350-2856
Fax: 022-2350-2857
E-mail:guanshan@yahoo.com

Jan 20th, 2013

Daniel Zheng
International Sales Department
Rainbow Pet Products Co., Ltd., Los Angeles, California.
1358 Westwood Blvd
Los Angeles, CA90024-4911
USA

Dear Mr. Zheng:

Re: "Rainbow" Brand Pet Products

Sincerely yours,
Tianjin Shangwen Import and Export Corp.
Guan Shan
Guan Shan (Mrs.)
Manager of Import and Export Department

Task 3 Making an Offer

An offer is a voluntary but conditional promise submitted by a buyer or seller (offeror) to another (offeree) for acceptance, and which becomes legally enforceable if accepted by the offeree. An offer is a clear indication of the offeror's willingness to enter into an agreement under specified terms, and is made in a manner that a reasonable person would understand its acceptance will result in a binding contract. Offers normally include a closing date, otherwise a period of 30 days after the date of offer is commonly assumed.

Student A plays a role as Daniel Zheng, the salesperson of the International Sales Department of Rainbow Pet Products Co., Ltd., Los Angeles, California.

Daniel Zheng makes an offer to Guan Shan, the manager of Import and Export Department, Tianjin Shangwen Import and Export Corp. on Jan. 25th, 2013. The price list is as follows (Table 8-2).

Table 8-2 Price List

Price List
Rainbow Pet Products Co., Ltd., Los Angeles, California
Dog Products Rainbow has multiple solutions for your dog's health needs.

Module Eight *Business Correspondence*

Categories	Item No.	Title	Description	Price USD CIF Tianjin
Categories	DM-101	Milk Replacer for Dogs	Milk Replacer for Dogs (Lg) Enriched with Colostrum Food Supplement for Puppies & Pregnant or Lactating Dogs Net Wt. 12 Oz. per box	16.00
	DM-102	Milk Replacer for Dogs (Lg)	Enriched with Colostrum Food Supplement for Puppies & Pregnant or Lactating Dogs Net Wt. 28 Oz. per box	38.00

Cat Products
Rainbow has multiple solutions for your cat's health needs.

Categories	Item No.	Title	Description	Remarks
Milk Replacer	CM-101	Milk Replacer for Cats Enriched with Colostrum	Food Supplement for Kittens & Pregnant or Lactating Cats Net Wt. 12 Oz. per box	12.00
Milk Replacer	CM-102	Milk Replacer for Cats	Enriched with Colostrum Food Supplement for Kittens & Pregnant or Lactating Cats Net Wt. 6 Oz. per box	5.00

 Make an offer with the following information.

- Opening sentence
- Makes an offer
- Delivery date and method of payment
- Valid time
- Closing sentence

(200-250 words)

Rainbow Pet Products Co., Ltd., Los Angeles, California.
1358 Westwood Blvd
Los Angeles, CA90024-4911
USA

Tel: 213-345-9125
Fax: 213-345-9125
E-mail:danielzheng@yahoo.com

Jan 25th, 2013

Import and Export Department
Tianjin Shangwen Import and Export Corp.
46 Weijin Road
Nankai District

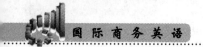

Tianjin 300071
China

Dear Mrs. Guan:

Re: "Rainbow" Brand Pet Products

Sincerely yours,
Rainbow Pet Products Co., Ltd., Los Angeles, California
Daniel Zheng
Daniel Zheng
International Sales Department

Task 4 Making a Counter-offer

Counter-offer is an offer given in response to an offer. It implies rejection of the original offer and puts the ball back in the court of the original offer who has three options: to accept it, expressly (by replying) or by implication (by not replying), issue another (counter-counter) offer, or reject it expressly.

Student B plays a role as Guan Shan, the manager of Import and Export Department of Tianjin Shangwen Import and Export Corp.

Guan Shan makes a counter-offer to Daniel Zheng on Feb. 1st, 2013, after receiving the offer. And he asks for 20% discount.

 Make a counter-offer with the following information.

- Opening sentence
- Express the reasons for not accepting
- Ask for 20% discount

- Closing sentence

(100-150 words)

Tianjin Shangwen Import and Export Corp.
46 Weijin Road
Nankai District
Tianjin 300071
China

Tel: 022-2350-2856
Fax: 022-2350-2857
E-mail:guanshan@yahoo.com

Feb 1st, 2013

Daniel Zheng
International Sales Department
Rainbow Pet Products Co., Ltd., Los Angeles, California.
1358 Westwood Blvd
Los Angeles, CA90024-4911
USA

Dear Mr. Zheng:

                    Re: "Rainbow" Brand Pet Products

Sincerely yours,
Tianjin Shangwen Import and Export Corp.
Guan Shan
Guan Shan (Mrs.)
Manager of Import and Export Department

Task 5 Accepting the Counter-offer

An acceptance letter is a confirmation for your willingness to accept the terms and conditions of a contract. You should do it within a particular time-frame which may vary between 1-3 months from the date of the sanction letter.

Student A plays a role as Daniel Zheng, the salesperson of the International Sales Department of Rainbow Pet Products Co., Ltd., Los Angeles, California.

Daniel Zheng accepts the counter-offer of Guan Shan, the Manager of Import and Export Department, Tianjin Shangwen Import and Export Corp. on Feb. 10th, 2013.

 Accept the counter-offer with the following information.

- Opening sentence
- Express acceptance
- Reasons for acceptance
- Notes
- Closing sentence

(100-150 words)

Rainbow Pet Products Co., Ltd., Los Angeles, California.
1358 Westwood Blvd
Los Angeles, CA90024-4911
USA

Tel: 213-345-9125
Fax: 213-345-9125
E-mail:danielzheng@yahoo.com

Feb. 10th, 2013

Import and Export Department
Tianjin Shangwen Import and Export Corp.
46 Weijin Road
Nankai District
Tianjin 300071
China

Dear Mrs. Guan:

Module Eight *Business Correspondence*

Re: "Rainbow" Brand Pet Products

Sincerely yours,

Rainbow Pet Products Co., Ltd., Los Angeles, California

Daniel Zheng

Daniel Zheng

International Sales Department

Encl: Contract

Task 6 Signing the Contract

A contract is a voluntary, deliberate, and legally binding agreement between two or more competent parties. Contracts are usually written but may be spoken or implied, and generally have to do with employment, sale or lease, or tenancy.

Student A plays a role as Daniel Zheng, the salesperson of the International Sales Department of Rainbow Pet Products Co., Ltd., Los Angeles, California.

Student B plays a role as Guan Shan, the manager of Import and Export Department of Tianjin Shangwen Import and Export Corp.

Daniel Zheng fills in the contract and send it enclosed in the acceptance letter. Guan Shan, the Manager of Import and Export Department, Tianjin Shangwen Import and Export Corp. signs the contract after receiving and returns one copy to Daniel Zheng.

Fill in the contract.

Contract

Contract No.: MN83601

Sellers:

Buyers:

China

This contract is made by and between the buyers and the sellers, whereby the buyers agree to buy and the sellers agree to sell the under mentioned commodity according to the terms and conditions stipulated below.

Style No.	Description	Quantity	Unit Price (CIF Tianjin)	Total
Total				

Packing: In wooden cases of 20 boxes each.

Insurance: To be covered by the sellers for 110% of the invoice value against All Risks as per CIC dated 1st Jan.,1981.

Port of shipment:

Port of destination:

Shipping mark: At sellers' option

Time of shipment: On _____, transshipment and partial shipment not allowed.

Terms of Payment: By irrevocable L/C at sight to reach the sellers 15 days before the date of shipment and to remain valid for negotiation in Los Angeles till the 15th days after the final date of shipment.

Documents: Full set negotiable clean on board ocean B/L in 3 originals and 3 copies;
          Signed commercial invoice in 3 originals and 3 copies;
          Packing list/weight memo in 3 originals and 3 copies;
          Certificate of quality, quantity and weight in 1 original and 3 copies;
          Original Certificate of Origin issued by Authorities in 1 original and 3 copies;;
          Insurance Policy in 3 originals and 3 copies;.

Guarantee of Quality: The Seller guarantee that the commodity thereof complies in all respects with the quality and specifications stipulated in this contract. The guarantee period shall be 6 years counting from the date on which the commodity arrives at the port of destination. Certificates of quality, quantity, weight, specifications and packing, etc. Issued by China Commodity Inspection Bureau (CCIB) located in the territory of the P. R. China shall be taken as final.

Claims: Within 90 days after the arrival of the goods at the destination port, should the quality, quantity, weight, specifications or packing be found not in conformity with the stipulations of this contract, or should any damages occurred by reason of quality within the guarantee period. The Buyer shall have the right to lodge a claim against the Seller. The Seller agrees to accept the certificate issued by CCIB located in the territory of the P. R. China as a claim document.

Force Majeure: In case of late delivery or non-delivery due to Force Majeure, the time of shipment might be duly extended, or alternatively a part or whole of this contract might be cancelled, but the Seller shall advise the Buyer of the occurrence mentioned above and send to the Buyer for its acceptance a certificate issued by the surveying institute where the accident occurs as evidence thereof within 14 days. In case the accident lasts for more than 4 weeks, the Buyer shall have the right to cancel this contract.

Late Delivery and Penalty: In case of late delivery, the Buyer shall have the right to cancel this contract, reject the goods and lodge a claim against the Seller. Except for Force Majeure, if late delivery occurs, the Seller must pay a penalty, and the Buyer shall have the right to lodge a claim against the Seller. The rate of penalty is charged at 0.5% for every 7 days, odd days less than 7 days should be counted as 7 days. The total penalty amount will not exceed 5% of the shipment value. The penalty shall be deducted by the paying bank or the Buyer from the payment.

Settlement of Disputes: Any dispute arising from or in connection with this contract shall be submitted to China Arbitration Commission for arbitration in accordance with its existing rules of arbitration. The arbitral award is final and binding upon both parties.

This contract is made in two original copies in English and becomes valid after signature, one copy to be each party in witness thereof.

Done and signed in Los Angeles on this 10th day of Jan., 2013.

Sellers: Buyers:

Task Process

Task 1　Writing a Promotion Letter

Rainbow Pet Products Co., Ltd., Los Angeles, California.
1358 Westwood Blvd
Los Angeles, CA90024-4911
USA

Tel: 213-345-9125
Fax: 213-345-9125
E-mail:danielzheng@yahoo.com

Jan 15th, 2013

Import and Export Department
Tianjin Shangwen Import and Export Corp.
46 Weijin Road
Nankai District
Tianjin 300071
China

Gentlemen:

Re: "Rainbow" Brand Pet Products

We have your name and address from the trade directory on the Internet.
We wish to inform you that we are dealing with all kinds of Pet's Products which enjoys good reputation, and shall be pleased to establish trade relations with you.
The catalog is enclosed which is showing various products being handles by our company with detailed description. Our products provide the nutrients necessary for a thriving, healthy young puppy/kitten.
If you are interested in our products, don't hesitate to enquire. Quotations will be sent upon receipt of your specific enquiry.
We are looking forward to your early reply with much interest.

Sincerely yours,
Rainbow Pet Products Co., Ltd., Los Angeles, California
Daniel Zheng
Daniel Zheng
International Sales Department

Encl: Catalog

Task 2 Writing an Enquiry

Tianjin Shangwen Import and Export Corp.
46 Weijin Road
Nankai District
Tianjin 300071
China

Tel: 022-2350-2856
Fax: 022-2350-2857
E-mail:guanshan@yahoo.com

Jan 20th, 2013

Daniel Zheng
International Sales Department
Rainbow Pet Products Co., Ltd., Los Angeles, California.
1358 Westwood Blvd
Los Angeles, CA90024-4911
USA

Dear Mr. Zheng:

Re: "Rainbow" Brand Pet Products

We have received your letter of Jan 15th, 2013 which enclosed the catalog of your "Rainbow" brand Pet Products.

We are interested in buying large quantities of Milk Replacers DM-101(10,000 boxes), DM-102(10, 000 boxes), CM-101(20, 000 boxes), CM-102(20,000 boxes) and should be obliged if you would give us a quotation per box CIF Tianjin.

We are big dealers in importing Pet Products in China. If you give us a favorable price, we will place big orders with you in the near future.

We are looking forward to your early reply with much interest.

Sincerely yours,
Tianjin Shangwen Import and Export Corp.
Guan Shan
Guan Shan (Mrs.)
Manager of Import and Export Department

Task 3　Making an Offer

Rainbow Pet Products Co., Ltd., Los Angeles, California.
1358 Westwood Blvd
Los Angeles, CA90024-4911
USA

Tel: 213-345-9125
Fax: 213-345-9125
E-mail:danielzheng@yahoo.com

Jan 25th, 2013

Import and Export Department
Tianjin Shangwen Import and Export Corp.
46 Weijin Road
Nankai District
Tianjin 300071
China

Dear Mrs. Guan:

Re: "Rainbow" Brand Pet Products

Thank you for your enquiry of Jan. 20th, 2013.
We are in position to offer you "Rainbow"Brand Pet Products as follows.

Dog Products				
Rainbow has multiple solutions for your dog's health needs.				
Categories	Item No.	Title	Description	Price USD CIF Tianjin
Milk Replacer	DM-101	Milk Replacer for Dogs	Enriched with Colostrum Food Supplement for Puppies & Pregnant or Lactating Dogs Net Wt. 12 Oz. per box	16.00
	DM-102	Milk Replacer for Dogs (Lg)	Enriched with Colostrum Food Supplement for Puppies & Pregnant or Lactating Dogs Net Wt. 28 Oz. per box	38.00
Cat Products				
Rainbow has multiple solutions for your cat's health needs.				

Module Eight Business Correspondence

Categories	Item No.	Title	Description	Remarks
Milk Replacer	CM-101	Milk Replacer for Cats Enriched with Colostrum	Food Supplement for Kittens & Pregnant or Lactating Cats Net Wt. 12 Oz. per box	12.00
Milk Replacer	CM-102	Milk Replacer for Cats	Enriched with Colostrum Food Supplement for Kittens & Pregnant or Lactating Cats Net Wt. 6 Oz. per box	5.00

And the delivery should be within 30 days after your placing an order with us. Payment of the purchase is to be effected by irrevocable L/C in our favor.

This offer is firm subject to your immediate reply which should reach us not later than Feb. 20th, 2013.

We are looking forward to your early reply.

Sincerely yours,
Rainbow Pet Products Co., Ltd., Los Angeles, California
Daniel Zheng
Daniel Zheng
International Sales Department

Task 4 Making a Counter-offer

Tianjin Shangwen Import and Export Corp.
46 Weijin Road
Nankai District
Tianjin 300071
China

Tel: 022-2350-2856
Fax: 022-2350-2857
E-mail:guanshan@yahoo.com

Feb 1st, 2013

Daniel Zheng
International Sales Department
Rainbow Pet Products Co., Ltd., Los Angeles, California.
1358 Westwood Blvd
Los Angeles, CA90024-4911

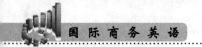

USA

Dear Mr. Zheng:

Re: "Rainbow" Brand Pet Products

Thank you for you offer on Jan. 25th, 2013, offering us Milk Replacers DM-101(10,000 boxes), DM-102 (10, 000 boxes), CM-101(20, 000 boxes), CM-102(20,000 boxes) at USD16 per box, USD38 per box, USD12 per box,USD5 per box CIF Tianjin respectively.

We regret to say that we find your price rather high.

We have a big market for Pet Products. Favorable price and friendly cooperation lead to our mutual and long-term interest of both companies. Should you be ready to reduce your price by 20% according to your offer, we might come to business.

We make you such a counter-offer: Milk Replacers DM-101(10,000 boxes), DM-102(10, 000 boxes), CM-101(20, 000 boxes), CM-102(20,000 boxes) at USD12.8 per box, USD30.4 per box, USD9.6 per box,USD4 per box CIF Tianjin respectively.

We are looking forward to your early reply.

Sincerely yours,
Tianjin Shangwen Import and Export Corp.
Guan Shan
Guan Shan (Mrs.)
Manager of Import and Export Department

Task 5 Accepting the Counter-offer

Rainbow Pet Products Co., Ltd., Los Angeles, California.
1358 Westwood Blvd
Los Angeles, CA90024-4911
USA

Tel: 213-345-9125
Fax: 213-345-9125
E-mail:danielzheng@yahoo.com

Feb. 10th, 2013

Import and Export Department
Tianjin Shangwen Import and Export Corp.
46 Weijin Road
Nankai District
Tianjin 300071

Module Eight Business Correspondence

China

Dear Mrs. Guan:

Re: "Rainbow" Brand Pet Products

We have received your Counter-offer of Feb. 1st, 2013, and we accept your price as an exception in order to welcome you as one of our customers.

We confirm supply of the goods, at the prices stated in your letter and are arranging for dispatch before March 1st, 2013. When the goods reach you, we feel confident you will be completely satisfied with them.

Enclosed is our Sales Contract in duplicate. Please sign and return one copy for our records.

We hope that our handling of your first order with us will lead to further business between us and mark the beginning of a happy working relationship.

Sincerely yours,
Rainbow Pet Products Co., Ltd., Los Angeles, California
Daniel Zheng
Daniel Zheng
International Sales Department

Encl: Contract

Task 6 Signing the Contract

Contract
Contract No.: MN83601

Sellers: Rainbow Pet Products Co., Ltd., Los Angeles, California.
1358 Westwood Blvd
Los Angeles, CA90024-4911
USA

Buyers: Tianjin Shangwen Import and Export Corp.
46 Weijin Road
Nankai District
Tianjin 300071
China

This contract is made by and between the buyers and the sellers, whereby the buyers agree to buy and the sellers agree to sell the under mentioned commodity according to the terms and conditions stipulated below.

Style No.	Description	Quantity	Unit Price (CIF Tianjin)	Total
DM-101	Milk Replacer for Dogs Enriched with Colostrum Food Supplement for Puppies & Pregnant or Lactating Dogs Net Wt. 12 Oz. per box	10,000 boxes	USD12.8 per piece	US$128,000
DM-102	Milk Replacer for Dogs (Lg) Enriched with Colostrum Food Supplement for Puppies & Pregnant or Lactating Dogs Net Wt. 28 Oz. per box	10,000 boxes	US$30.4 per piece	US$304,000
CM-101	Milk Replacer for Cats Enriched with Colostrum Food Supplement for Kittens & Pregnant or Lactating Cats	20,000 boxes	USD9.6 per box	US$192,000
CM-102	Milk Replacer for Cats Enriched with Colostrum Food Supplement for Kittens & Pregnant or Lactating Cats Net Wt. 6 Oz. per box	20,000 boxes	USD4.0 per box	USD80,000
Total	USD704,000(SAY US DOLLARS SEVEN HUNDRED AND FOUR THOUSAND ONLY) CIF Tianjin			

Packing: In wooden cases of 20 boxes each.

Insurance: To be covered by the sellers for 110% of the invoice value against All Risks as per CIC dated 1st Jan.,1981.

Port of shipment: Los Angeles, USA

Port of destination: Tianjin, China

Shipping mark: At sellers' option

Time of shipment: On March 1st, 2013, transshipment and partial shipment not allowed.

Terms of Payment: By irrevocable L/C at sight to reach the sellers 15 days before the date of shipment and to remain valid for negotiation in Los Angeles till the 15th days after the final date of shipment.

Documents: Full set negotiable clean on board ocean B/L in 3 originals and 3 copies;
    Signed commercial invoice in 3 originals and 3 copies;
    Packing list/weight memo in 3 originals and 3 copies;
    Certificate of quality, quantity and weight in 1 original and 3 copies;
    Original Certificate of Origin issued by Authorities in 1 original and 3 copies;;
    Insurance Policy in 3 originals and 3 copies;.

Guarantee of Quality: The Seller guarantees that the commodity thereof complies in all respects with the quality and specifications stipulated in this contract. The guarantee period shall be 6 years counting from the date on which the commodity arrives at the port of destination. Certificates of quality, quantity, weight, specifications and packing, etc. Issued by China Commodity Inspection Bureau (CCIB) located in the territory of the P. R. China shall be taken as final.

Claims: Within 90 days after the arrival of the goods at the destination port, should the quality, quantity, weight, specifications or packing be found not in conformity with the stipulations of this contract, or should any damages occurred by reason of quality within the guarantee period. The Buyer shall have the right to lodge a claim against the Seller. The Seller agrees to accept the certificate issued by CCIB located in the territory of the P. R. China as a claim document.

Force Majeure: In case of late delivery or non-delivery due to Force Majeure, the time of shipment might be duly extended, or alternatively a part or whole of this contract might be cancelled, but the Seller shall advise the Buyer of the occurrence mentioned above and send to the Buyer for its acceptance a certificate issued by the surveying institute where the accident occurs as evidence thereof within 14 days. In case the accident lasts for more than 4 weeks, the Buyer shall have the right to cancel this contract.

Late Delivery and Penalty: In case of late delivery, the Buyer shall have the right to cancel this contract, reject the goods and lodge a claim against the Seller. Except for Force Majeure, if late delivery occurs, the Seller must pay a penalty, and the Buyer shall have the right to lodge a claim against the Seller. The rate of penalty is charged at 0.5% for every 7 days, odd days less than 7 days should be counted as 7 days. The total penalty amount will not exceed 5% of the shipment value. The penalty shall be deducted by the paying bank or the Buyer from the payment.

Settlement of Disputes: Any dispute arising from or in connection with this contract shall be submitted to China Arbitration Commission for arbitration in accordance with its existing rules of arbitration. The arbitral award is final and binding upon both parties.

This contract is made in two original copies in English and becomes valid after signature, one copy to be each party in witness thereof.

Done and signed in Los Angeles on this 10th day of Jan., 2013.

Sellers:	Buyers:
Rainbow Pet Products Co., Ltd.	Tianjin Shangwen Import and Export Corp.
Los Angeles, California.	
Daniel Zheng	Guan Shan
Daniel Zheng	Guan Shan
International Salesperson	Manager of Import and Export Manager

Knowledges

Theories of International Trade

Mercantilism (1500—late 1700) is a theory holding that it was essential for a nation to accumulate a stock of precious metals contributed by Thomas Mun (1571-1641), who wrote England's Treasure by Foreign Trade which is called the bible of mercantilism.

Absolute Advantage explains the process by which the markets and production actually operate in society, and it holds that it is market forces, not governments, that should determine the direction, composition and volume of international trade. Each nation should specialize in producing those goods that it could produce most efficiently (had an absolute advantage). Adam Smith (1723-1790) is the father of economics who wrote An Inquiry into the Nature and Causes of the Wealth of Nations (1776) which is called the bible of free trade movement.

Comparative Advantage is a theory that further expands on the absolute advantage. It holds that even though a nation has an absolute disadvantage in the production of two or more products, it still has a comparative advantage in producing the product(s) in which its absolute disadvantage is less. David Richardo (1772-1817) is the main contributor of comparative advantage with his works-*Principles of Political Economy and Taxation*.

Practice: Fill A-C into Column II.

I	II Key features
Mercantilism	
Absolute Advantage	
Comparative Advantage	

A: Specializing in producing those that a country has more absolute advantage or disadvantage

B: Government controlled international trade

C: Division of labor and specialization

Globalization

Globalization is the system of interaction among the countries of the world in order to develop the global economy. Globalization refers to the integration of economics and societies all over the world. Globalization involves technological, economic, political, and cultural exchanges made possible largely by advances in communication, transportation, and infrastructure.

Effects of Globalization are as follows.

1. Improvement of International Trade. Because of globalization, the number of countries where products can be sold or purchased has increased dramatically.

2. Technological Progress. Because of the need to compete and be competitive globally, governments have upgraded their level of technology.

3. Increasing Influence of Multinational Companies. Often, the head office is found in the country where the company was established.

Practice: Fill A-M into Column I or II.

I Positive Effects of Globalization	II Negative Effects of Globalization

A: In order to cut down costs, many firms in developed nations have outsourced their

Module Eight *Business Correspondence*

manufacturing and white-collar jobs to Third-World countries like India and China, where the cost of labor is low.

B: One of the most visible effects is the improved quality of products due to global competition.

C: Globalization has led to an increase in activities such as child labor and slavery.

D: Globalization has resulted in a fiercely-competitive global market, and unethical practices in business is a by-product of this.

E: Foreign Direct Investment that flows into the developing countries.

F: The people of developing countries can obtain gainful employment opportunities.

G: Globalization may have inadvertently helped terrorists and criminals.

H: All the industrial waste is accumulated and pollution levels are sky-high.

I: One of the most powerful effects of globalization is the spread of education.

J: While the rich are getting richer, the poor are struggling for a square meal.

K: The spread of know-how can also be expanded to, which has spread far and wide.

L: The world that we live in today is a result of several cultures coming together.

M: Pollution has severely impacted the quality of air that we need so very much for our survival.

 Skills Requirements

Vocabulary: International Organization

 Fill in the full name of the international organization.

EU	
IMF	
ISO	
UN	
WTO	

Listening: Free Trade Zone

 Listen to the passage twice, Choose the best answer according to what you have listened.

1. Free Trade Zone is an area where goods may be traded without any barriers imposed by customs authorities like quotas and tariffs.

    A. True   B. False   C. Not mentioned

2. There were around 3000 free trade zones across 116 countries in the year 1995.

 A. True   B. False   C. Not mentioned

3. The Purpose of Free Trade Zone is to increase the foreign exchange earnings and decrease the employment opportunites.

 A. True   B. False   C. Not mentioned

4. FTZs prove to be beneficial not only for the importers but also for the exporters.

 A. True   B. False   C. Not mentioned

5. Free Trade Zone caused the increasing of unemployment in the developed country.

 A. True   B. False   C. Not mentioned

Speaking: Trade Control

Work in pairs with a partner. Look at the question. Take one minute to prepare your answer. Think of reasons to explain your choice. Then tell your partner your answer and reasons.

WHAT IS THE MOST IMPORTANT REASONS FOR TRADE CONTROL?

- Job protection
- Health and safety protection
- National security

Reading: Benefits of International Trade

Read the passages below. And choose the best answers.

Benefits of International Trade[1]

 International trade has flourished over the years due to the many benefits it has offered to different countries across the globe.

 International trade is the 1. _____ of services, goods, and capital among various countries and regions, without much hindrance. The international trade 2. _____ for a good part of a country's gross 3. _____ product. It is also one of important sources of revenue for a developing country.

 With the help of modern production techniques, highly advanced transportation systems, transnational corporations, outsourcing of manufacturing and services, and rapid industrialization, the international trade system is growing and spreading very fast.

 International trade among different countries is not a new concept. History suggests that in the past there were several instances of international trade. Traders used to transport silk, and spices through the Silk Route in the 14th and 15th century. In the 1700s fast sailing 4. _____ called Clippers, with special crew, used to transport tea from China, and spices from Dutch East Indies to different European countries.

---

1. Based on http://www.economywatch.com/international-trade/benefit.html.

Module Eight *Business Correspondence*

The economic, political, and social significance of international trade has been theorized in the 5. _____ Age. The rise in the international trade is essential for the growth of globalization. The restrictions to international trade would limit the nations to the services and goods produced within its territories, and they would lose out on the valuable revenue from the global trade.

The benefits of international trade have been the major drivers of growth for the last half of the 20th century. Nations with strong international trade have become prosperous and have the power to control the world economy. The global trade can become one of the major contributors to the 6. _____ of poverty.

David Ricardo, a classical economist, in his principle of comparative advantage explained how trade can benefit all parties such as individuals, companies, and countries involved in it, as long as goods are produced with different relative costs. The net benefits from such activity are called 7. _____ from trade. This is one of the most important concepts in international trade.

Adam Smith, another classical economist, with the use of principle of absolute advantage demonstrated that a country could benefit from trade, if it has the least absolute cost of production of goods, i.e. per unit input yields a higher volume of output.

According to the principle of comparative advantage, benefits of trade are dependent on the opportunity cost of production. The 8. _____ cost of production of goods is the amount of production of one good reduced, to increase production of another good by one unit. A country with no absolute advantage in any product, i.e. the country is not the most competent producer for any goods, can still be benefited from focusing on export of goods for which it has the least opportunity cost of production.

Benefits of International Trade can be reaped further, if there is a considerable decrease in barriers to trade in agriculture and manufactured goods.

- Enhances the domestic competitiveness.
- Takes advantage of international trade technology.
- Increase sales and profits.
- Extend sales potential of the existing products.
- Maintain cost competitiveness in your domestic market.
- Enhance potential for expansion of your business.
- Gains a global market share.
- Reduce dependence on existing markets.
- Stabilize seasonal market fluctuations.

1. A. communication   B. exchange   C. purchase
2. A. accounts   B. applies   C. responsible
3. A. international   B. local   C. domestic
4. A. planes   B. cars   C. ships
5. A. Information   B. Industrial   C. Modern
6. A. reduction   B. increasing   C. creation
7. A. losts   B. gains   C. costs
8. A. opportunity   B. competitive   C. total

Writing: Claim and Settlement

 Reply the following letter with the following information.

- Opening
- Express apology
- Accept the requirement
- Closing

(50-100 words)

Big Star Office Stationary Co. Ltd., N.Y.

528 East 80th Street Row   Tel: +1 212 794 4689
New York, NY 10075   Fax: +1 212 794 4688
USA

May 12th, 2013

Huang Shan
Export Manager
Beijing Zhenghe Trade Co., Ltd.
24 Suzhou Hutong
Zhongcheng District
Beijing 10005
China

Dear Sirs,

We regret to inform you that the 300 cartons of A4 Paper under order No. 356899 you shipped on April 24, 2013 were badly damaged by moisture.

We are now writing to you to change the packing terms for our order No.356911 which will be shipped in May in order to avoid the damage in the future.

200 pieces wrapped with moisture-proof paper in a plastic bags, 500 bags in a carton. All the cases must be strong enough to stand rough handling and ocean transportation. The name of the importer, order No. should be marked in English.

We are looking forward to your acceptance.

Yours sincerely,
Big Star Office Stationary Co. Ltd., N.Y.
James Simpson
James Simpson
Import Manager

Module Eight *Business Correspondence*

Beijing Zhenghe Trade Co., Ltd.

24 Suzhou Hutong   Tel: +86 010 6495 3278
Zhongcheng District   Fax: +86 010 6495 3274
Beijing 10005
China

May 20th, 2013

James Simpson
Import Manager
Big Star Office Stationary Co. Ltd., N.Y.
528 East 80th Street Row
New York, NY 10075
USA

Dear Sirs,

Yours sincerely,
Big Star Office Stationary Co. Ltd., N.Y.
Huang Shan
Huang Shan
Export Manager

附　录
Appendix

Keys to Module 1

Leading In

Keys:

OVER 60 POINTS:

Others see you as someone they should "handle with care." You're seen as vain, self-centered, and who is extremely dominant. Others may admire you, wishing they could be more like you, but don't always trust you, hesitating to become too deeply involved with you.

51 TO 60 POINTS:

Others see you as an exciting, highly volatile, rather impulsive personality; a natural leader, who's quick to make decisions, though not always the right ones. They see you as bold and adventuresome, someone who will try anything once; someone who takes chances and enjoys an adventure. They enjoy being in your company because of the excitement you radiate.

41 TO 50 POINTS:

Others see you as fresh, lively, charming, amusing, practical, and always interesting; someone who's constantly in the center of attention, but sufficiently well-balanced not to let it go to their head. They also see you as kind, considerate, and understanding; someone who'll always cheer them up and help them out.

31 TO 40 POINTS:

Others see you as sensible, cautious, careful and practical. They see you as clever, gifted, or talented, but modest. Not a person who makes friends too quickly or easily, but someone who's extremely loyal to friends you do make and who expect the same loyalty in return. Those who really get to know you realize it takes a lot to shake your trust in your friends, but equally that it takes you a long time to get over if that trust is ever broken.

21 TO 30 POINTS:

Your friends see you as painstaking and fussy. They see you as very cautious, extremely careful, a slow and steady plodder. It would really surprise them if you ever did something impulsively or on the spur of the moment, expecting you to examine everything carefully from every angle and then, usually decide against it. They think this reaction is caused partly by your careful nature.

UNDER 21 POINTS:

People think you are shy, nervous, and indecisive, someone who needs looking after, who always wants someone else to make the decisions &who doesn't want to get involved with anyone or anything! They see you as a worrier who always sees problems that don't exist. Some people think you're boring. Only those who know you well know that you aren't.

Knowledges

Practice: Fill A-L into Column II.

Keys:

I	II
International Trade	G K
FDI	A C L J
License	B E I
Franchise	D H
Contract management	F

Practice: Match column I with column II.

Keys:

    1-D 2-A 3-E 4-B 5-C

Skills Requirements

Vocabulary: Abbrieviation

Keys:

abbr.	English	Chinese	abbr.	English	Chinese
1. ad.	advertisement	广告	11. Co.	company	公司
2. m-f	Monday-Friday	从周一到周五	12. corp	corporation	（有限）公司
3. dept.	department	部	13. P/T	part time	非全日制
4. Jr.	junior	初级	14. F/T	full time	全日制
5. Sr.	senior	资深	15. temp.	temporarily	临时性工作
6. Wpm	words per minute	打字/每分钟	16. perm.	permanent	永久性的
7. ref	Reference	推荐信	17. k	1000	一千
8. blvd	Boulevard	大道，林荫大道	18. Ave.	avenue	街道
9. O/T	over time	超时，加班	19. Fr. Ben.	fringe benefits	额外福利
10. CV	Curriculum vitae	简历	20. Etc.	et cetera	等等

1. He is responsible for checking and calculating staff for their <u>O/T</u>.

2. He opened a fashion house in the Fifth <u>Ave</u>.

3. Virtually all of the <u>Sr</u>. Managers at our company were promoted from <u>Jr</u>. Managers within.

4. His future is closely bound up with that of the <u>Co</u>.

5. I learned about it from your <u>Ad</u>. in the newspaper.

6. In only a few weeks, my average reading speed went from roughly 300 <u>Wpm</u>, to over 800.

7. EDC <u>Co</u>. and DHF <u>Co</u>., were amalgamated into a <u>corp</u>.

8. Candidate shall send a letter of application with a <u>CV</u> to the HR manager.

9. You can work anytime for 1-3 hours a day, <u>m-f</u>. Or You can get 3 working days a week as long as you can do equivalent task.

10. Do you have skills (musician, carpenter, writer, <u>etc</u>.) that you can use to get some part time jobs?

11. The applicant provides a portfolio of work, <u>ref</u>, and arranges for a preliminary screening (probably a phone interview).

12. Whether it's a <u>P/T</u> or <u>F/T</u> job, embrace it.

13. Next to each <u>dept</u>. is its location and the name of the manager.

14. Most of the workers who work <u>temp</u>. came from all over the country.

15. I have a <u>perm</u>. and stable job here.

16. The store is located on Sunset <u>Blvd</u> in West Hollywood.

Listening: Job Advertisement

 Tapescript:

Job Advertisement

Shenzhen Nanshan Textiles Import and Export Corp. Requires Documentation Specialist.

Shenzhen Nanshan Textiles import and Export Corp. specialized in exporting textiles to European market. College degree and 2 years relevant experience is required. Have excellent computer skills including knowledge of common Office software. Compensation is negotiable.

If you think you have the ability and the confidence, please contact with Wang Wenli. The telephone number is 0755-26486001. The address is Shenzhen Nanshan Textiles Import and Export Corp. 2045 Nanshan Avenue, Nanshan District, Shenzhen 518052, China.

Appendix

Keys:

Company Name	Shenzhen Nanshan Textiles Import and Export Corp.
Job Title	Documentation Specialist
Products	Textiles
Education required	College degree
Experience required	2 years relevant experience
The Salary	Negotiable
Contact person	Wang Wenli

Speaking: Tips for Writing an Application Letter
Keys: Free

Reading: Job Description for a Sales Manager
Keys:
    1. C 2. B 3. A 4. A 5. B 6. C 7. B 8. A 9. C 10. B

Writing: Application Letter
Keys:

SHENZHEN POLYTECHNIC
No. 4089, West Shahe Road
Xili Lake
Nanshan District
Shenzhen 518055
China

Feb. 26th, 2013

HR Department
Shenzhen Nanshan Textiles import and Export Corp.
2045 Nanshan Avenue
Nanshan District
Shenzhen 518052
China

Gentlemen:

I'm applying for the position of sales representative as advertised in China Daily on Feb. 26th, 2013.

I graduated from Shenzhen Business School. I hold a certificate in Sales and I am prepared to undergo further training if necessary. I have benn working as a sales representative for Huashan Groups for two years. Please find my enclosed résumé in support of my application.

I am confident in my skills and my previous work experience will enable me to perform the duties of the position well. I am available for an interview at a time convenient to you and can be contacted by telephone on 136-8973-6543.

I'm looking forward to your early reply.

Yours sincerely,
Wang Xiaohua
Wang Xiaohua

Encl: CV

Keys to Module 2

Leading In

Keys:

    1. A 2. A 3. B 4. A 5. B 6. C 7. A

Practice: Tell the process of communication according to chart 2-1 in your own words.

Keys:

    The sender has an idea, encodes the idea into message and then he selects a channel to convey the message. The receive accepts the messages, decodes the message into understanding and uses feedback to respond. The communication process happens in a specific context and may be influenced by any kinds of noises.

Knowledges

Practice: Match column I with column II.

Keys:

    1-B 2-A 3-B 4-A 5-B 6-B 7-B 8-A

Practice: Match column I with column II.

Keys:

    1-C 2-C 3-A 4-B 5-C 6-B 7-B 8-B 9-A 10-A 11-C 12-A 13-A

Skills Requirements

Practice: Selecting the best channel from table 2-1

Appendix

Keys:
    1. Face to face   2. Telephone   3. Voice-mail   4. Fax
    5. Team Meeting   6. Video Conferencing   7. Memo
    8. Letter   9. Report

Vocabulary: Work Categories
Keys: Free

Listening: Interviews

 Tapescript:

Interviews

1. Interviewer: Can you give us a brief introduction of yourself in two minutes? Go for it.

Interviewee: With my qualifications and experience, I feel I am hardworking, responsible and persuasive. Your organization could benefit from my communication and interpersonal skills.

Question: Which one is not mentioned in the interview?

2. Interviewer: Give me a summary of your current job description.

Interviewee: I have been working as a computer programmer for five years. To be specific, I do system analysis, trouble shooting and provide software support.

Qestion: How many years has the interviewee been working as a computer programmer?

3. Interviewer: Why did you leave your last job?

Interviewee: I feel I have reached the "glass ceiling" in my current job.

Question: Why did the interviewee leave his last job?

4. Interviewer: How would your friends or colleagues describe you?

Interviewee: They say Mr. Chen is an honest, hardworking and responsible man who deeply cares for his family and friends.

Question: What kind of person is Mr. Chen?

5. Interviewer: What contribution did you make to your previous organization?

Interviewee: I have finished three new projects, and I am sure I can apply my experience to this position.

Question: How many projects has the interviewee finished?

Keys:
    1. B 2. D 3. B 4. D 5. C

Speaking: Interview Etiquette
Keys: free

Reading: Sina Claims Lead in China's Micro-blog Market

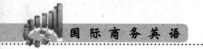

Keys:

1. B 2. A 3. C 4. B 5. B

Writing: Thank-you Email after an Interview

Keys:

From: emilybrown@yahoo.com
Date: Sept. 26, 2012
To: abccoltd@yahoo.com
Cc:
Subject: Interview
Mr. Lee Thank you for interviewing me this morning to discuss the sales representative position. I enjoyed our conversation, and I am very excited about the possibility of joining your team. You mentioned that strong "people" skills are the most important factors, and this is an area in which I am good at.
The enclosed are the reference from my supervisor who has said, "Emily Brown is one of the hardest-working students I have known." Thank you for considering me for this exciting opportunity. As you requested, I'm enclosing a list of professional references. Please feel free to call me if you need additional information. Thank you for your time, and I look forward to hearing from you. Best Regards Emily Brown

Keys to Module 3

Leading In

Keys:

What's your E.Q. (Entrepreneurial Quotient)?

If you scored +35 or more, you have everything going for you. You ought to achieve spectacular entrepreneurial success (barring acts of God or other variables beyond your control).

If you scored +15 to +34, your background, skills and talents give you excellent chances for success in your own business. You should go far.

If you scored 0 to +15, you have a head start of ability and/or experience in running a business and ought to be successful in opening an enterprise of your own if you apply yourself and learn the necessary skills to make it happen.

If you scores 0 to -15, you might be able to make a go of it if you ventured on your own, but you would have to work extra hard to compensate for a lack of built-in advantages and skills that give others a leg up in beginning their own business.

If you scored -15 to -43, your talents probably lie elsewhere. You ought to consider whether building your own business is what you really want to do, because you may find yourself swimming against the tide if you make the attempt. Another work arrangement—working for a company or for someone else, or developing a career in a profession or an area of technical expertise—may be far more congenial to you and allow you to enjoy a lifestyle appropriate to your abilities and interests.

Knowledges

Practice: Match Column I with Column II.

Keys:

1-C 2-B 3-E 4-D 5-C 6-F 7-D 8-C 9-B 10-A 11-A

Practice: Match Column I with Column II.

Keys:

1-B 2-G 3-A 4-D 5-E 6-F 7-A 8-G 9-B 10-E 11-B 12-G 13-A 14-D 15-C

Skills Requirements

Vocabulary: Office Facilities

Keys:

Office Furniture	desk/chair 桌椅 swivel chair 旋转椅 (desk) lamp 桌灯 stationery cupboard 文具柜 notice board 通知板	lectern 讲台 (book) shelf 书架 filing cabinet 文件柜 wastepaper basket/bin 垃圾桶 board marker 门牌
Office Equipment/ Facilities	shredder 碎纸机 telephone 电话机 carousel socket 旋转式幻灯放映机 photocopier 影印机 laser/inkjet printer 激光打印机 franking machine 加盖"邮资已付印证的自动邮资盖印机 computer (pC)/ desktop 桌上电脑 VDU (visual display unit) 视频显示器 microphone 麦克风 overhead projector 投影机 cassette(tape) recorder(player) 录音机 video cassette recorder (VCR) 录像机 digital video camera 摄像机	typewriter 打字机 answering machine 电话答录机 remote control 遥控器 calculator 计算器 slide projector 幻灯机

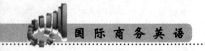

Office Stationary	scissors 剪刀　　　　　　　　　　　stapler 订书机
	staple 订书钉　　　　　　　　　　　in tray/in box 收信盒
	out tray/out box 发信盒　　　　　　paper clip 回形针
	pencil holder 笔架
	(electric) pencil sharpener 电子卷笔刀
	(ball point) pen/Biro 圆珠笔　　　rubber/eraser 橡皮
	elastic band/rubber band 橡皮圈　notepad 便笺
	notebook 笔记本　　　　　　　　　message pad 便笺
	desk diary 桌历　　　　　　　　　　headed paper 带信头的信纸
	appointment diary 日历
	phone book/telephone directory/yellow pages 电话号码簿
	typing paper 打字纸　　　　　　　　printer paper 打印纸
	file/folder 文件　　　　　　　　　　window envelope 开窗信封
	flip chart 挂图

Listening: Asking for Directions

Tapescript:

Asking for Directions

1.

Mary: Where are we on this map now?

Tom: We are here. We are at this crossroads.

Mary: I'm afraid I'm lost. How can we go to the largest department store in the city.

Tom: I think we should take the left side road at the crossroads. And then Head straight up the street towards west about two blocks.

Question: Where is the department Store?

2.

Jerry : Excuse me. Could you tell me how to get to the shopping mall from here?

Emily: Walk along the Cherry Avenue and you can see it on the left. It's between the Post Office and Bank.

Jerry : Thank you very much.

Emily: It's my pleasure.

Question: Where is the Bank?

3.

Owen: Would you please tell me if there is a hospital nearby?

Susan: Go along the street until you come to the second traffic lights, turn to the right and walk three blocks. It is just over there.

Owen: Is it far from here?

Susan: It is only about 15 minute's to walk.

Question: Which sentence is right?

4.

Jack: Do you know where the Simpson Hall is?

Chris: Simpson Hall is on the corner of Bellflower Boulevard and Atlantic Avenue.

Jack: How can I get there?

Chris: It is three miles from here. You'd better take a taxi.

Jack: OK, I will.

Question: How can Jack go to the Simpson Hall.

5.

Ben: Excuse me? I think I'm lost. Can I go from here to the Holiday Inn?

Xiaoming: You can take a No.407 bus here, then get off at the second stop, and you will see a big sign of the Holiday Inn. You can't miss it

Ben: Could you please tell me how to get to the station at first?

Xiaoming: Ok, I will go there with you.

Question: Which sentence is right?

Keys:

1. A   2. C   3. C   4. A   5. C

Speaking: First Day at Work

Keys: Free

Reading: Starting a New Job

Keys:

Do	Don't
Put on the one suit that you know makes you shine.	Shouldn't make lewd hand gestures anywhere.
Leave plenty of time to get there early.	Do not utter these words: "That's not how we did it at my old company."
Your work day begins when you leave your house.	Don't contribute to the grapevine.
Walk in with a smile on your face.	Don't complain about your boss, your office mate, any co-workers, or your previous job.
Introduce yourself to those you meet	don't neglect any assigned work.
Keep your head up and remember to make eye contact.	
Be polite and friendly to everyone you encounter.	
Ask questions.	
Smile a lot and be friendly.	
Use your lunch hours to get together with your current co-workers.	
Figure out who has the authority to give you work to do.	
Pay attention to the grapevine.	
Continue to arrive early.	
Volunteer for projects.	

Writing: Note

Keys:

> Sharon:
>
> I have an appointment with a client. I'll be back after three hours. If Mr. Johnson calls for me, please explain where I am and ask him send us the catalogues and instructions of the office equipment.
>
> Thanks
>
> Tom

Keys to Module 4

Leading In

Keys:

If you answered "yes" on 17 or more of these questions, look at your paycheck (if you are lucky enough to still get one). If the company that issued the check isn't owned by you, it is time for some soul searching: Do you have debts to pay? Kids in college? Alimony? Want to take it easy? Maybe better to wait. Do you have a little extra cash in the bank and several credit cards? Do you have a spouse, partner, friends, or kids who will cheer you on? If so, start thinking about what kind of business you want to set up. It doesn't matter what age you are: research by the Kauffman Foundation shows that more and more over–50s are setting up their own businesses. Talk to people who have made the plunge, learn how to plan and deliver a product or service, think about that small business you might buy, talk to people with whom you would like to work, and talk to customers.

"I like to take risks" is not on the list. People don't choose to be entrepreneurs by opting for a riskier lifestyle. What they do, instead, is reframe the salary vs. entrepreneur choice as between two different sets of risk: the things they don't like about having a steady job — such as the risk of boredom, working for a bad boss, lack of autonomy, lack of control over your fate, and getting laid off — and the things they fear about being an entrepreneur — possible failure, financial uncertainty, shame or embarrassment, and lost investment. In the end, people who are meant to be entrepreneurs believe that their own abilities (e.g. leadership, resourcefulness, pluck, hard work) or assets (e.g. money, intellectual property, information, access to customers) significantly mitigate the risks of entrepreneurship. Risk is ultimately a personal assessment: what is risky for me is not risky for you.

"I want to get rich" is not on the list either. All else being equal (and all else is rarely equal in the real world), on the average, people who set up their own businesses don't make more money, although a few do succeed in grabbing the brass ring. But the "psychic benefits" — the challenge, autonomy, recognition, excitement, and creativity — make it all worthwhile.

Appendix

Knowledges

Practice: Make a comparison of Five Business Structure Alternatives.

Keys:

	Owner	Limited Liability	Legal and administration costs	Private or Public	Field
SP	Member(one)	No	Lowest	Private	Small Business
Partner	Partner(two or more)	No	Lower	Private	Lawyer Consultant Accountant
LLC	Member(one or more)	Yes	High	Private	Small and medium Business
Inc.	Shareholder	Yes	Higher	Public	Big Business
PLC	Shareholder	Yes	Highest	Public	Big Business

Practice: Match Column I with Column II.

Keys:

    1-C 2-A 3-F 4-B 5-D 6-E

Practice: Have a group discussion on the Global 2011 and 2010 compared with 2012 above. And answer the following questions according to Table 4-5.

Keys: Free

Practice: Fill in the form with letter A to U.

Keys:

Introduction (A seed is planted.)	D Q R S
Growth (It begins to sprout.)	A E F I K
Maturity (It shoots out leaves and puts down roots as it becomes an adult)	C G M O P T U
Decline (The plant begins to shrink and die out.)	B H J L N

Fill in the form with letter A to G.

Keys:

Level 1 Core Product	B D G
Level 2 Actual Product	C F
Level 3 Augmented Product	A E

Skills Requirements

Vocabulary: Company

Keys:

1. Royal Dutch Shell Plc 荷兰皇家壳牌公司
2. Exxon Mobil Corp 埃克森美孚；美孚公司；艾克森美孚；美孚石油公司
3. BP Plc 英国石油公司
4. Wal-Mart Store, Inc. 沃尔玛百货公司
5. China National Petroleum Company 中国石油天然气总公司
6. Sinopec Group 中国石油化工集团
7. State Power Grid Corp 中国国家电网公司
8. Chevron Corp 雪佛龙；雪佛龙公司；雪佛龙石油公司；雪弗龙
9. ConocoPhillips Company 康菲石油公司
10. Toyota Motor Corp 丰田汽车公司

Keys:

1. Columbia Broadcasting System（CBS） 哥伦比亚广播公司
2. British Nuclear Associates 英国核子联合公司
3. Independent Design House（IDH） 独立设计公司
4. China Southern Airlines 中国南方航空公司
5. Atlantic Container Line 大西洋集装箱海运公司
6. China Youth Travel Service（CYTS） 中国青年旅行社
7. China Ocean Shipping Agency（COSA） 中国外轮代理公司
8. Windsor House Shopping Center 皇室大厦购物中心
9. 3M China Limited Guangzhou Branch Office 3M中国有限公司广州分公司

Vocabulary: Products and Services

Keys:

1-B 2-A 3-B 4-A 5-A 6-B 7-B 8-B 9-B 10-A

Listening: Wal-Mart Stores Inc.

 Tapescript:

Wal-Mart Stores Inc.

Wal-Mart Stores Inc. is the world's biggest retailer and also the biggest employer with over 2.1 million full- and part-time workers worldwide — 1.4 million in the U.S. It is also one of the world's most valuable companies.The company is the world's third largest public corporation, according to the Fortune Global 500 list in 2012.

Known for its low pricing and wide selection of goods, Wal-Mart has become the undisputed king of retailing. It is an American multinational retailer corporation that runs chains of large discount department stores and warehouse stores.

The company was founded by Sam Walton in 1962, incorporated on October 31, 1969, and publicly traded on the New York Stock Exchange in 1972. It is headquartered in Bentonville, Arkansas. The company was guided by founder Sam Walton's passion for customer satisfaction and "Every Day Low Prices".Wal-Mart remains a family-owned business, as the company is controlled by the Walton family who own a 48% stake in Wal-Mart.

Wal-Mart has 8,500 stores in 15 countries, under 55 different names. The company operates under the Wal-Mart name in the United States. Wal-Mart's investments outside North America have had mixed results: its operations in the United Kingdom, South America and China are highly successful, whereas ventures in Germany and South Korea were unsuccessful.

Wal-Mart reported sales of $443.9 billion for fiscal 2012, an increase of 5.9% from the previous year. Wal-Mart stores in the U.S. generated $264.1 billion in sales — a 1.5% increase from the previous year — while Sam's Club reported $53.7 billion in revenues for a 8.8% increase. International stores led the company in growth with $125.8 billion in revenue, a 15.2% increase. Net income for the entire company was $15.6 billion in fiscal 2012.

Keys:

    1. B   2. A   3. C   4. B   5. B   6. A   7. C   8. A

Speaking: Establishing a Company

Keys: Free

Reading: IKEA

Keys:

    1. B   2. D   3. C   4. A

Writing: Company Profile of McDonald's Plaza

Keys:

> McDonald's Plaza is the world's leading food service organization. We operate over 30,000 restaurants in more than 100 countries on six continents.
>
> Since its incorporation in 1955, McDonald's Corporation by Ray Kroc has become the world's largest quick-service restaurant organization. Systemwide sales totaled more than $46 billion in 2003.

Keys to Module 5

Leading In

Keys:

    A: Ideas Person

    B: Manager

    C: Investigator

D: Team worker

E: Expert

F: Policemen

Knowledges

Practice: Think about how you usually act in teams. Complete these tables. Compare your answers with those from others in your team.

Keys: free

Practice: Fill in the blank with A-L.

Keys:

	International Marketing	International Sales
Starting Point:	K: Market	D: Factory
Focus:	G: Customer Needs	A: Existing Product
Means:	H: Integrated Marketing	C: Selling and Promoting
Process:	B: One to many	I: Usually one to one
Horizon:	J: Longer term	E: Short term
Ends:	L: Profits through Satisfaction	F: Profits through Volume

Practice: Fill A-P into Column II.

Keys:

I	II
Product	C F H I J L M O
Price	B
Promotion	D E G I K P
Place	A N

Practice: Choose the best answer from A, B and C.

Keys:

    1. A   2. C   3. B   4. C

Skills Requirements

Vocabulary: Needs, Wants and Demands

Keys:

    1-B   2-C   3-A   4-D

Vocabulary: Marketing Terms

Keys:

    1-B   3-C   3-E   4-A   5-F   6-D

Vocabulary: Charts Description

Keys:

↗	advance, ascend, rise, gain, increase, progress, raise, mount, enlarge, expand, extend, flourish, get up, go up, grow, catch up, add to
↘	decrease, compress, curtail, cut, diminish, lessen, reduce, shorten
→↓	drop, dive, lapse, descend, decline, destroy, collapse, ruin, fall, defeat, overthrow, plunge, tumble, give up
→↘↗	come around, get back, get better, heal, improve, reclaim, regain, recover, revive, recuperate, retrieve, rescue
↗→	even, flat, constant, horizontal, level off, remain steady, smooth
∧	peak at, at the top of
∨	at the bottom of
WW	vary irregularly, rise and fall, increase and decrease, undulate, wave, move in waves or with a smooth, wavelike motion, have a wavelike appearance/face/form, have a wavy line or appearance

Listening: Marketing Mix of Subway

 Tapescript:

Marketing Mix of Subway

Subway is a multinational restaurant franchise that mainly sells sandwiches and salads. It is the modern version of fast food restaurant in which each sandwich is made in front of the customer according to his or her taste. It basically is a consumer driven product.

The prices of all of the items offered by Subway seem to be very reasonable and in accordance with the target market segments. Pricing of Subway is 'Strength' for Subway and in most of the markets it has penetrating pricing strategy.

Most of the Subway outlets around the world are in commercial areas. The part of the area being crowded most of the time can be an advantage for Subway. People roaming around for the purpose of shopping can actually be expected to step in and make a purchase at Subway. It may be a possibility that the presence of the shopping area add to the sales of Subway.

Considering the promotional activities being carried out by Subway, it is quite obvious that right now subway is not taking any kind of initiatives to promote itself. There are no advertisements on television, in the form of print ads or on radio, as opposed to some of its competitors like McDonalds and KFC.

Keys:

    1. B   2. A   3. B   4. B   5. B

Speaking: Bar Chart

Keys: free

Reading: Employment of Canada

Keys:

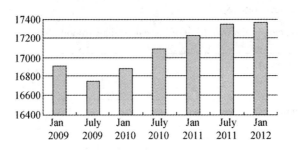

Writing: Line Chart

Keys:

    This chart demonstrates the figures of sales of hamburgers in Harry's in 1998. As we can see from the chart, the sales changed greatly throughout the year. As is shown in the graph, the sales of hamburgers in Jan, Feb. and March kept almost unchanged, around 2,000 each month, in spite of a slight decrease in April and May, when about 1800 were sold each month. From June on, there appeared a steady rise of sales, which amounted to 2600 in July and 3000 in August, the highest point during the whole year. Then after August, the figure fell down steeply and bottomed out in October, arriving at 1200, despite a small rebound in November and December, which was 1900 and 2000 respectively. From the statistics shown in the graph, we can see that the sales were the highest in August in Harry's and the lowest in October in the year 1998.

Keys to Module 6

Leading In

Keys:

    1. A business meal is not a time to relax and "let loose". It is a test of your social skills and your level of sophistication. Your interpersonal skills, including your treatment of the wait staff, are on display. One of the biggest blunders at the business meal is alcohol abuse. You can undo months and years of good impressions by excessive drinking. The key point to remember is that "business" should always be the number one item on the menu.

    2. The boss's name should be said first. Proper introductions have a pecking order with the person of rank, honor, or importance being mentioned first. The other person is being introduced

or presented to the person of honor. Follow these three steps. One, say the name of the key person. Two, mention the name of the other person and say something about him or her. Three, come back to the key person and say something about him or her. Here is an example where the boss is Mike Williams and the spouse is Cindy Clark.

"Mike, I would like to introduce my wife, Cindy Clark. Cindy is an interior decorator. Mike Williams is our company president."

Think of book-ending the introduction with the person of importance.

3. True, clothing is never neutral. Some people disagree and say; "I don't judge a book by its cover." Maybe, this is true. However, people do judge you. If you are at a business holiday party, remember the key word is "business." Dress how you want when with your family and friends. Women should avoid wearing clothes that are too tight, too short, or too sexy.

4. False. A man does not have to wait for a woman in business to extend her hand for a handshake. Business should be gender neutral. Many men were taught to wait for a woman to extend her hand in social settings. Note that the etiquette for handshakes varies around the world. So, if you are traveling to other countries or are meeting international clients, check the protocol for handshaking.

5. False. Your drink should be held in your left hand so your right hand is free for handshaking. This also prevents your right hand from being cold and damp.

6. Your salad plate is to the left of the entrée plate. An easy way to remember this is to think of the BMW car. From left to right, think Bread, Meal, Water. Bread and all food to the left of the plate are yours. Water and all drinks to the right of the plate are yours. Knowing this will help you avoid taking the wrong bread, eating the wrong salad, and drinking from the wrong water glass.

7. Yes, please tell an associate if she has spinach in her teeth. An important part of etiquette is kindness.

8. If you need to excuse yourself during a meal, place your napkin on your chair.

While eating, people do not want to see a dirty napkin with food stains. When the meal is complete and people are leaving the table, place the napkin to the left of the plate.

9. BBQ ribs are not a good meal option at a company banquet. You need to keep your hands and face clean. Remember that this is not your "Last Supper". Eat ribs on your own time and with your family and friends. The best advise for "difficult to eat" foods is to not order them at a business meal.

10. Pushing back your plate is not the signal indicating that you have finished eating. Think of your plate as a clock. Put your fork and knife in the 10 and 4 o'clock positions with the top of the utensils pointing at the number 10 and the base of the utensils at the number 4. The knife should be on the outside with its blades facing inward towards the fork.

Use these tips to help you project a professional and credible image in any business setting. These ideas will help develop relationships without worrying about etiquette blunders you may be making.

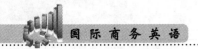

Knowledges

Practice: True or False

Keys:

1. F 2. T 3. T 4. T 5. F 6. T 7. F 8. T

Practice : Choose the best answer.

Keys:

1. B. It's not a cup of coffee, for heaven's sake. And don't slurp, either.

2. D. It's more polite not to call attention to the fact that you can't drink champagne.

3. D. Leave it on your chair. Definitely don't put it on the table--what if you have crumbs on it?

4. B. Indicating where your guest should sit will make her feel more comfortable.

5. D. Call and set up another appointment. And don't forget to apologize for your error. Imagine how you'd feel if it was you!

Skills Requirements

Vocabulary: Gesture

Keys:

I	II
1. The thumb-up sign	Good and Great
4. The thumb-down sign	Disapproval and angry
5. The "V" sign	Victory
6. The single finger beckon	Coming here

Listening: Dinner Etiquette

 Tapescript:

Dinner Etiquette

A: Once seated, unfold your napkin and use it for occasionally wiping your lips or fingers. At the end of dinner, leave the napkin tidily on the place setting.

B: Start eating before a signal from the host to do so.

C: Use one's bread for dipping into soups or mopping up sauces.

D: Serve the lady sitting to the right of the host first, then the other ladies in a clockwise direction, and lastly the gentlemen.

E: Talking with one's mouth full.

F: Hold the knife and fork with the handles in the palm of the hand, forefinger on top, and thumb underneath.

G: Stretch across the table crossing other guests to reach food, wine or condiments.

H: Always make a point of for their hospitality before leaving.

I: Leave some food to one side of your plate if you feel as though you have eaten enough.

On the other hand, don't attempt to leave your plate so clean that it looks as though you haven't eaten in days!

Keys:

I	II
Do	A D F H I
Don't	B C E G

Speaking: Invitation

Keys:Free

Reading: Apple Stock Up On Positive Early Reviews For iPhone 5

Keys:

    1. B   2. A   3. A   4. A   5. B

Writing: Invitation Card

Keys:

> Mr. and Mrs. James Stanley
> Request the pleasure of your company
> At Welcome Dinner
> Sunday Evening, Jan. 20th, 2013
> At half past nineteen
> Kowloon Shangri-la Hotel
> 64 Mody Road, Tsim Sha Tsui East, Kowloon, HK

Keys to Module 7

Leading In

Keys:

There are many styles that you can adopt when negotiating. One is the hard or aggressive negotiator in which you believe the "more for you means less for them". If there is a fixed pie available you will see your role as getting the largest slice of it.

If you answered true to six or more of the above statements, your adopted style is probably of the 'hard' bargainer.

By your behaviour you are competitive and see nothing wrong with doing everything you can to weaken the other party by bluffs:

    "We have other options"

    "We will sue for penalties and damages"

    "We have another client anxious to sign with us this afternoon"

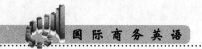

Other manipulative ploys are: preconditions, phoney offers, tough guy soft guy, take it or leave it etc. All styles have different dimensions and the aggressive negotiator has two ways of showing him/herself

Knowledges

Practice: True or False

Keys:

    1. T   2. F   3. T   4. F   5. T   6. T   7. F   8. T   9. T   10. T

Practice: Fill A-L into Column II.

Keys:

I	II Advantages
Host-court negotiation	A C G H
Guest-court negotiation	D F I K
Third-place negotiation	B E J L

Fill A-F into Column II.

Keys:

I	II Disadvantages
Oral Negotiation	B D F
Written Negotiation	A C E

Skills Requirements

Vocabulary: Incoterms

Keys:

Incoterm	Loading on truck (carrier)	Export-Customs declare	Carriage to port of export	Unloading of truck in port of export	Loading charges in port of export	Carriage to port of import
EXW	Buyer	Buyer	Buyer	Buyer	Buyer	Buyer
FCA	Seller	Seller	Seller	Buyer	Buyer	Buyer
FAS	Seller	Seller	Seller	Seller	Buyer	Buyer
FOB	Seller	Seller	Seller	Seller	Seller	Buyer
CFR	Seller	Seller	Seller	Seller	Seller	Seller
CIF	Seller	Seller	Seller	Seller	Seller	Seller
DAT	Seller	Seller	Seller	Seller	Seller	Seller
DAP	Seller	Seller	Seller	Seller	Seller	Seller
CPT	Seller	Seller	Seller	Seller	Seller	Seller
CIP	Seller	Seller	Seller	Seller	Seller	Seller
DDP	Seller	Seller	Seller	Seller	Seller	Seller

Appendix

Incoterm	Unloading charges in port of import	Loading on truck in port of import	Carriage to place of destination	Insurance	Import customs clearance	Import taxes
EXW	Buyer	Buyer	Buyer	Buyer	Buyer	Buyer
FCA	Buyer	Buyer	Buyer	Buyer	Buyer	Buyer
FAS	Buyer	Buyer	Buyer	Buyer	Buyer	Buyer
FOB	Buyer	Buyer	Buyer	Buyer	Buyer	Buyer
CFR	Buyer	Buyer	Buyer	Buyer	Buyer	Buyer
CIF	Buyer	Buyer	Buyer	Seller	Buyer	Buyer
DAT	Seller	Buyer	Buyer	Seller	Buyer	Buyer
DAP	Seller	Seller	Seller	Seller	Buyer	Buyer
CPT	Seller	Seller	Seller	Buyer	Buyer	Buyer
CIP	Seller	Seller	Seller	Seller	Buyer	Buyer
DDP	Seller	Seller	Seller	Seller	Seller	Seller

Listening: Business Negotiation

 Tapescript:

Business Negotiation

1. Mr. Black: Is that Mr. Anderson speaking? This is Black from London.

Mrs. Anderson: Oh, hi, Mr. Black! How is everything going?

Mr. Black: Not so well. Mr. Anderson, I think you know what happened to the goods we have ordered from you.

Mrs. Anderson: Yes, we have received your e-mail.

Mr. Black: As you know, 30% cartons are damaged. Would you like to find a way to solve the problem?

Mrs. Anderson: We are trying to find out what caused the problem.

Mr. Black: The Christmas is coming. Our customers are looking forward to the goods.

Mrs. Anderson: Take it easy. If the problem was caused by us, we'll pay for your loss.

Question: What happened to the goods?

2. Mr. Black: How is your investigation about the outdated Orange Juice?

Miss Hu: Well, the problem was caused by mislabeling. Some workers used the old labels for the new products.

Mr. Black: Do you mean the Orange Juice is not outdated, but the labels are?

Mr. Anderson: That's right. We will send your company new labels.

Mr. Black: But who pays for our loss?

Miss Hu: Our company will pay all the extra expenses for relabeling.

Question: Who will pay for the loss?

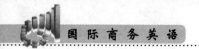

3. Mr. Guo: It seems to me that USD150 per piece is rather high. Would you like to reduce the prices by 20%

Mrs. Chen: It would be very difficult to reduce them by 20%, I'm afraid. But there's a good chance of reducing them by 15%.

Mr. Guo: Can't you make it cheaper?

Mrs Chen: This is the lowest possible price. We're selling at cost already.

Mr. Guo: OK, I'll accept it.

Question: What is the price?

4. Mrs. Winters: Mr. Liu, how about making Dalian the port of destination instead of Qingdao?

Mr. Liu: Mrs. Winters, I'm afraid we can't agree to this. Our clients are in Qingdao. And it will also add considerably to the expenses.

Mrs. Winters: We have no choice. If you insist, we have to wait until December.

Mr. Liu: No, it's too late. Time is crucial.

Mrs. Winters: I think it is worth trying if transshipment to Dalian will help you catch the season demand.

Mr. Liu: Your idea may be a good one, but who will pay for the freight from Dalian to Qingdao?

Mrs. Winters: On our accounts.

Mr. Liu: That will be no problem.

Question: Who will pay for the freight from Dalian to Qingdao?

5. Mr. Zheng: Miss Bush, we would suggest that for this particular order you let us have a D/A.

Miss Bush: Mr. Zheng, we regret we cannot accept it.

Mr. Zheng: How about payment by D/P?

Miss Bush: Sorry, I'm afraid I can't agree with you there.

Mr. Zheng: To tell you frankly, we do have a cash flow problem this year. Could you make an exception and kindly make easier payment terms?

Miss Bush: Sorry, we cannot accept your suggestion. It's our regular practice to pay by L/C.

Question: Which one can be accepted by Miss Bush?

Keys:

1. B 2. B 3. B 4. A 5. C

Speaking: Urging L/C

Keys:

Mr. Ma: Hello, can I speak to Mr. Smith?

Mr. Smith: This is Smith speaking.

Mr. Ma: Hi, Mr. Smith. This is Ma. We wish to draw your attention to the fact that the date of delivery of your Order No.5790 is approaching. But we haven't received your covering letter of credit yet.

Mr. Smith: Really? Sorry. I'm too busy recently. I will get it done right away and then I'll call you immediately. The date of shipment will not be delayed. I'm sorry to bring inconvenience to you because of the L/C.

Mr. Ma: The goods are ready for dispatch for quite some time. Please do your utmost to expedite the L/C.

Mr. Smith: No problem.

Mr. Ma: Please see to it that the L/C stipulations conform strictly to the terms of the contract so as to avoid subsequent amendment.

Mr. Smith: Of course.

Mr. Ma: OK. Look forward to your good news. Bye.

Mr. Smith: Bye.

Reading: There's More to Negotiate than Just the Price
Keys:
1. B 2. A 3. B 4. C 5. A 6. B 7. C 8. A

Writing: Order
Keys:

From: xinhuatextiles@yahoo.com
Date: Sept. 26th, 2013
To: stevenjones@yahoo.com
Cc:
Subject: Order
Mr. Jones Thank you for your order of Sept. 25th, 2013. We regret to say that we can not accept your order at present. Unfortunately we are out of stock of the items you ordered. And we don't know when the manufacturers can supply the goods. We are sorry not to be able to meet your order. If you are interested in other items in our catalog, don't hesitate to tell us. Best Regards, Mary Wood

Keys to Module 8

Leading In

Keys:

Part 1

If you scored mostly a) responses for these items, you are high in conscientiousness. A conscientious person is someone who has a high degree of self-control and perseverance. Conscientious traders are good rule-followers, and they often do well trading mechanical systems. Traders who are low in conscientiousness will have difficulty following explicit rules and often trade more discretionarily. Ideally, you want a style of trading that is more structured and detail-oriented if you are more conscientious. Trying to trade in a highly structured manner will only frustrate a trader who is low in conscientiousness. Such a trader would do better with big picture trades that do not require detailed rules and analysis. Similarly, very active trading with rigid loss control will come easier to the conscientious trader; less frequent trades with wider risk parameters will come easier to the trader lower in conscientiousness.

Part 2

If you scored mostly a) responses for these items, you are relative high in neuroticism. The trader prone to neuroticism tends to experience more emotional interference in his or her trading. Wins can create overconfidence; losses can create fear and hesitation. The trader who is low in neuroticism is more likely to react to trading problems with efforts at problem solving and analysis. He or she will not take wins or losses particularly personally. Neuroticism is a mixed bag when it comes to trading. Often the person who is high in neuroticism is emotionally sensitive and can use this sensitivity to obtain a gut feel for market action. The trader who is low in neuroticism may experience little emotional disruption with trading, but may also be closed off to subtle, intuitive cues when a trade starts to go sour. In my recent experience, I have been surprised at how successful gut traders are often relatively neurotic traders. Very active trading methods are particularly challenging for such traders, as they don't allow much time for regaining emotional equilibrium after losses. This can lead to cascades of losses and significant drawdowns of equity. It is much easier for the non-neurotic trader to turn losses around, since these are less likely to be tied to self-esteem.

Part 3

If you scored mostly a) responses for these items, you are a relatively risk-averse trader. Trading with careful stops and money management, and trading smaller time-frames where risk can be controlled with the holding period will come most naturally for the risk-averse trader. The risk-seeking trader is one who enjoys stimulation and challenge. Larger positions and longer holding periods are easier to tolerate for the risk-seeking trader. Very often, the risk-seeking trader will be impulsive in entering trades and will have difficulty trading during periods of boredom (low volatility). The risk-averse trader often experiences difficulty hanging onto winning trades and will cut profits short to avoid reversals. This trader will be challenged during periods of high market volatility. Position sizing is key and often overlooked as a trading variable. Trading too small will bore the risk-seeking trader, who will then lose focus. Trading too large will overwhelm the risk-averse trader, who will also then lose focus.

Knowledges

Practice: Fill A-C into Column II.

Keys:

I	II Key features
Mercantilism	B
Absolute Advantage	C
Comparative Advantage	A

Practice: Fill A-M into Column I or II.

Keys:

I Positive Effects of Globalization	II Negative Effects of Globalization
B E F I K L	A C D G H J M

Skills Requirements

Vocabulary: International Organization

Keys:

EU	EUROPEAN UNION
IMF	INTERNATIONAL MAONETARY FUND
ISO	INTERNATIONAL STANDARD ORGANIZATION
UN	UNITED NATIONS
WTO	WORLD TRADE ORGANIZATION

Listening: Free Trade Zone

 Tapescript:

Free Trade Zone

Free Trade Zone, popularly known as FTZ, is a special designated area within a country where normal trade barriers like quotas, tariffs are removed and the bureaucratic necessities are narrowed in order to attract new business and foreign investments.

There were around 3000 free trade zones across 116 countries in the year 1999, where nearly 43 million people were working. These FTZs produce various goods such as shoes, clothes, sneakers, toys, convenient foods items, electronic goods, etc. The other important purposes of such trade zones are the development of export-oriented units, increase in the foreign exchange earnings, and generation of employment opportunities.

The main idea behind creation of free trade zones is to facilitate cross-border trade by removing obstacles imposed by customs regulations. Free trade zones ensure faster turnaround of planes and ships by lowering custom related formalities. FTZs prove to be beneficial both for the importers and exporters, as these zones are designed to reduce labor cost and tax related expenditures. Free trade zones help the traders to utilize the available business opportunities in the best possible way. FTZs promote export-oriented industries. These zones also help to increase foreign exchange earnings. Employment opportunities created by free trade zones help to reduce unemployment problem in the less developed economies.

Keys:

    1. A   2. B   3. B   4. A   5. C

Speaking: Trade Control

Keys: Free

Reading: Benefits of International Trade

Keys:

    1. B   2. A   3. C   4. C   5. B   6. A   7. B   8. A

Writing: Complain and Settlement

Keys:

Beijing Zhenghe Trade Co., Ltd.

24 Suzhou Hutong	Tel: +86 010 6495 3278
Zhongcheng District	Fax: +86 010 6495 3274
Beijing 10005	
China	

                        May 20th ,2013

James Simpson
Import Manager
Big Star Office Stationary Co. Ltd., N.Y.
528 East 80th Street Row
New York, NY 10075
USA

Dear Sirs,

Referring to your letter of May 12th, 2013, we regret to hear that the goods are damaged. We may accept you special packing requirements on condition that you agree to pay the extra charges.

Your opinions on packing will be passed on to our manufacturers. I'm sure the new packing will give you satisfaction.

We believe we can conclude the business by our mutual efforts.

Yours sincerely,
Big Star Office Stationary Co. Ltd., N.Y.
Huang Shan
Huang Shan
Export Manager

参考文献
References

[1] Michael R. Czinkota, Ilkka A. Ronkainen, Michael H. Moffett. International Business [M]. The 7th Edition. Beijing: China Machine Press, 2010.

[2] Arthur A. Thompson Jr., A. J. Strickland III, John E.Gamble, Crafting and Executing Strategy: The Quest for Competitive advantage, Concepts and Cases [M]. The 15th Edition. Beijing: China Machine Press, 2009.

[3] Philip Kotler, Gary Armstrong. Principles of Marketing [M].The 12th Edition. Beijing: Tsinghua University Press, 2009.

[4] Lan Wood, Catrin Lioyd-Jones, Anne Williams. Pass Cambridge BEC Preliminary [M]. The 2nd Edition. Beijing: Economic Science Press, 2002.

[5] Lan Wood, Paul Sanderson, Anne Williams, Catrin Lioyd-Jones. Pass Cambridge BEC Vantage [M]. The 2nd Edition. Beijing: Economic Science Press, 2002.

[6] Rolf Cook, Mara Pedretti, Helen Stephenson. Success with BEC Preliminary[M]. The 3nd Edition. Beijing: Economic Science Press, 2008.

[7] James S. O'Rourke. The Business Communication Casebook [M]. The 1st Edition. Peking University Press, 2005.

[8] Robert March. International Team Negotiation [M]. The 1st Edition. UIBE Press, 2009.

[9] 严明.商务沟通[M].北京：科学出版社，2010.

[10] 严明.大学英语跨文化交际教程[M].第1版.北京：清华大学出版社，2009.

[11] 庄恩平.跨文化商务沟通[M].北京:首都经济贸易大学出版社，2011.

[12] 王维波，车丽娟.跨文化商务交际[M].北京：外语教学与研究出版社，2008.

[13] 窦然，苏丽文，罗树民.国际商务谈判[M].上海：复旦大学出版社，2012.

[14] 庞岳红.商务谈判[M].北京：清华大学出版社，2011.

[15] 吴思乐，胡秋华.世纪商务谈判英语口语[M].大连：大连理工出版社，2007.

[16] 郭淳凡.进出口作业英文信函格式范例[M].广东：广东经济出版社，2003.

[17] 程斌，崔峥. 商务英语应用文模板大全[M]. 济南：山东科学技术出版社, 2009.

[18] 朱文忠，周杏英. 实用商务谈判英语[M]. 北京：对外经济贸易大学出版社，2007.

[19] 张达球，周岩，陈宜平. 会展英语[M]. 北京：化学工业出版社，2007.

[20] 卢小金. 参展商实务[M]. 大连：东北财经大学出版社，2010.

[21] 陈岩，刘玲. 国际贸易实务[M]. 北京：对外经济贸易大学出版社，2007.

[22] 浩瀚，等. 商务英语谈判高频话题[M]. 北京：中国水利水电出版社，2009.

[23] 徐美荣. 外贸英语函电[M]. 第2版. 北京：对外经济贸易大学，2007年.

[24] 刘慧玲，王俊. 国际商务函电[M]. 北京：北京大学出版社，2002.

[25] 刘嵩，曲丽君. 纺织服装外贸英语函电[M]. 北京：中国纺织出版社，2008.

[26] 罗凤翔，杜清萍. 国际商务英语模拟实训教程[M]. 北京：中国商务出版社，2005.